KEN MILES

by Art Evans

a scrapbook
with remembrances from
Charlie Agapiou, Bernard Cahier,
Peter Miles, John Morton, Al Moss, Augie Pabst,
Joe Playan, Bill Pollack, Carroll Shelby,
Dick Van Laanen, Cy Yedor and Carol Zipper

KEN MILES

by Art Evans

FIRST EDITION

Library of Congress Card Catalog Number: LC 2004 135251

ISBN 0-9705073-3-X

Published by Photo Data Research, LLC (SAN: 297-4010)
800 South Pacific Coast Highway
Redondo Beach, California 90277-4700 USA
Phone (310) 540-8068, Fax (310) 373-5988
E-mail: photodataresearch@yahoo.com

Printed in the United States of America

Very special thanks to Jim Sitz plus John and Ginny Dixon for their diligent work checking facts and discovering mistakes. Thanks also to my talented cousin, David Evans (who is more like my older brother) for his editing. Thanks to Dick Sherwin for archival photographs from the *Sports Car Journal* and many members of the Fabulous Fifties Association for the donation of materials. Other assistance was provided by Charlie Agapiou, Casey Annis, *Road & Track* Librarian Jane Barrett, John Beazley, Phil Binks, Walter R. Haessner of the Aztex Corporation, *Road & Track* Editor Tom Bryant, Bernard Cahier, Ron Ellico, Betsy Evans, Shav Glick, Dr. Mike Jacobsen, Ron Kellogg, Allen Kuhn, Mike Lynch, John Markoeta (who found Peter Miles for me), Peter Miles, Bob Norton, Warren Olson, Joe Playan, Bill Pollack, Carroll Shelby, Harold Treichler, Bob Tronolone, Cy Yedor and my distant cousin, Bob Evans, for data regarding Cobras and Shelby American.

Photo Credits: A large number of photographs have been donated by members to the archives of The Fabulous Fifties Association. In many cases, photographs donated or loaned are from family collections and there was no evidence as to the identification of the individuals who actually took the photographs. Nevertheless, every possible attempt has been made to ascertain who the photographers were and to give them credit. If any errors of omission or misidentifications have been made, sincere apologies are herewith extended.

Racing photographs from past eras are available from Bernard Cahier (www.F1-photo.com), Dave Friedman (davestills@aol.com), Ron Kellogg (562-693-0950), Allen Kuhn (www.vintage-sportscar-photos.com) and Bob Tronolone (818-432-6038).

Cover photograph by Allen Kuhn

INTRODUCTION

Ken Miles was my hero and my friend. Through the haze of passing years, I cannot, for the life of me recall when we got acquainted.

I do remember the first time I saw him race, however. The date was January 24, 1954. My uncle had just purchased a new Austin Healey 100. He asked me if I would like to go with him for a short trip. Uncle Phil's marriage was childless and he was my mother's only brother, so we were close.

Our destination was Palm Springs. When we arrived, my uncle took me to see my very first sports car race. While (or whilst as Ken would have said) there, I caught a disease from which I never recovered. Ken Miles in his little MG Special won the under-1500cc semi-main going away in a field of, would you believe, 67 cars.

In those days, the first five finishers in the semi-main were invited to run with the big dogs. There was no qualifying then and grid positions were determined by drawing numbers out of a hat. Those from the semi-main were gridded last. Threading his way through all that heavy iron, Miles ended up third overall behind Sterling Edwards in his 4.1 Ferrari and Chuck Daigh in a Jaguar Special. To take the third spot, Ken had passed, among others, Bill Pickford in his Jaguar Special, a Kurtis-Cadillac, a Cad-Allard and Howard Wheeler in his 212 Ferrari!

For the balance of 1954, I became a dedicated spectator and started taking photographs with my Rolleiflex. Unfortunately, none of these early images have survived various moves, but I do know that I went out of my way to shoot Ken. Whilst (There it is again!) doing so, somehow or another, we struck up a friendship that lasted for the rest of his life.

I am fully aware that all who came into contact with Ken Miles didn't necessarily have smooth sailing. Even though he lacked much formal education, he was highly intelligent and didn't suffer fools. One of his failings, I think, in personal relationships, was that he would often let the fool know about his foolishness.

A number of those with whom Ken had affiliations, particularly in business, didn't come away with a particularly high opinion of him.

I was fortunate that our relationship was always and solely social. After we became acquainted, we took to going out to dinner together. Ken was always with Mollie and I was usually with my current paramour. In later years, the Miles and Evans families became close and for the last ten years of Ken's life, he and my father were best friends as were my stepmother, Betsy, and Mollie.

Looking back on the many times we were together, I cannot recall very much discussion about racing or cars. In those days, I was studying for my masters degree in political science and going to law school. The conversations I recall were about politics and history. Ken was widely read on a great variety of subjects. And he was quite a decent writer too. If he hadn't been so impatient with school as a youth, his life might have taken quite a different path.

In later years, I have become fascinated with our experiences during what we now call the fabulous fifties of sports car racing. So far, I have written three books about the subject and have accumulated an archive of data.

Early on, I started to gather materials on Ken. The data grew and grew, so eventually I sorted things in chronological order and started to digitize everything on my computer's hard disk.

I never intended to write a biography. It's rather obvious from my previous efforts that formal biography is not my forte. So what we have here is sort of an annotated scrapbook.

One of the first tasks I tackled was a birth to death chronology of major happenings. It was initially intended to be an appendix. But since the format doesn't seem to lend itself to a table of contents, I moved the chronology to the front so that you, dear reader, can have an overview for reference purposes. If you want to examine a particular aspect of Ken's life, locate it in the chronology and this will give you a good idea as to where to look in the book.

I could have included a lot more material than has ended up on these pages. If this were a scrapbook for individual remembrance, it would have many more pages. But printing costs money and the bigger the book, the more it costs. So I have been selective regarding what to include in order that the final product will be somewhat affordable. I hope that everyone who has an interest in Ken and his life will be able to acquire a copy.

KEN MILES CHRONOLOGY

November 1, 1918: Kenneth Henry J. Miles born, Sutton Coldfield, England. Father: Eric Miles, mother: Clarice Jarvis

1929:At age 11, Ken rides 350cc trials motorcycle and crashes.

1933: At age 15, he meets and vows to marry Mollie. Builds Austin 7 Special; Mollie paints it BRG. Quits high school. Apprenticed to Wolseley Motors; works way up from janitor to fabricating to assembly.

September 1939: Joins British Territorial Army; posted to anti-aircraft unit.

1940: Becomes an Army driver-training instructor at Blackpool.

1942: Marries Mollie. Sent to Royal Corps of Electrical and Mechanical Engineers School. Promoted to staff sergeant.

June 26, 1944: D-Day+1; Lands at Normandy in a tank unit. On through France, Holland, Belgium and finally, Germany.

January 1946: Discharged from the Army. Returns to Wolseley Motors as a toolmaker. Buys a Frazer-Nash; installs a Ford V8-60 engine. Enters hill climbs and club races.

1947: Ken and Mollie live at 29, Queenswood Road, Moseley, Birmingham. Ken buys a Type 40 Bugatti (s/n 40497).

1948: Crashes in the Frazer-Nash, destroying the car. Hired at Morris Motors as a development engineer. Goes to Webley & Scott in the research and development department. Works with John Rawley building 500cc specials; company fails. Peter Miles is born.

December 1951: Goes to the U.S. to accept employment as service manager at Gough Industries.

July 20, 1952: Runs his first race in U.S. in an MG-TD owned by Gough Industries. Competes in a number of other races in the MG. Plans and starts to build his first MG Special, R-1.

April 19, 1953: Enters R-1 and wins at Pebble Beach in the under-1500cc semi-main event. Goes on to win the under-1500cc semi-main event at every single race entered in 1953.

1954: Elected president of the California Sports Car Club. Plans and starts to build his second MG Special, R-2, the "Shingle." Sells R-1 to Cy Yedor. Drives a stock MGTF for Gough Industries, the Troutman-Barnes Special and a Formula III Cooper while building R-2.

1955: Re-elected president of the Cal Club.

February 13, 1955: Runs R-2 in its first outing at Willow Springs; is DNF due to teething troubles.

March 4, 1955: Leaves Gough Industries and goes to work for Clem Atwater Sports Cars in sales and service. Now known as "Mr. MG."

June 11-12, 1955: Miles and co-driver, Johnny Lockett, place 12th overall at Le Mans in MG EX182 entered by MG Cars Ltd., GB.

December 1955: Quits Clem Atwater and goes to work for John Von Neumann's Competition Motors as field representative.

January 14, 1956: Wins his first race in a Porsche for John Von Neumann. Continues to successfully race Porsche Spyders for Von Neumann. With Dick Van Laanen, designs Paramount Ranch and lays out Pomona on the Los Angeles County Fairgrounds parking lot.

August 6, 1956: Sets speed records at Bonneville.

November 17 and 18, 1956: Enters the Porsche-Cooper for the first time at Paramount Ranch; scores a clean sweep: first on Saturday in the under-1500cc semi-main; on Sunday first in the semi-main and the main event. Sets all-time lap record.

December 7, 1956: Takes the Porsche-Cooper to Nassau finishing second in the semi-main and fourth in the main event against stiff European and East Coast competition.

1957: Elected president of the Cal Club for a third term.

February, 1957: The Porsche factory forces John Von Neumann to sell the Porsche-Cooper, putting Miles back in a Spyder.

September 21, 1957: The Cal Club stages the first event at the new Riverside Raceway. John Von Neumann is in Europe and left word that Ken was not to drive in von Neumann's absence. Ken very angry!

November 5, 1957: Ken announces he is leaving Ecurie Von Neumann at the end of the year.

February 9, 1958: Enters his first race for Otto Zipper in the Porsche 550RS at Pomona (2nd overall in under-1500 main).

1959: Goes to work for Universal Auto Corp. as sales manager. Ken and Mollie become naturalized American citizens.

May 28, 1960: Opens his own shop in North Hollywood.

October 16, 1960: Runs his first race in a Dolphin Formula Junior at Riverside for the Dolphin Engineering Co.

1961: Becomes the Sports Car Club of American U.S. Road Racing Champion. Starts to campaign a production Sunbeam-Alpine for the importer, Rootes Motors. Comes in second in the F-Production Pacific Coast Championship.

1962: Miles' shop closed by the government for not paying taxes.

1963: Elected a board member of the California Sports Car Club Region of the SCCA.

February 1963: Goes to work for Shelby American. Appointed competition manager.

1964: Re-elected as a board member of the CSCC Region of the SCCA.

February 28, 1965: Comes in first overall at the 2000-KM of Daytona in a Shelby American Ford GT40 with co-driver Lloyd Ruby.

February 5 and 6, 1966: Miles and Ruby first overall at the 24-Hours of Daytona in a Shelby GT40 Ford MkII.

March 26, 1966: First overall at the 12-Hours of Sebring in a Shelby Ford MkII X1 Roadster.

June 19, 1966: Comes in second at the 24-Hours of Le Mans in a Shelby GT40 Ford MkII

August 1: Ken and Mollie have dinner at the Portofino Inn, Redondo Beach, with Art Evans Jr.

August 17, 1966: Killed at Riverside testing a Ford J-Car prototype.

August 21, 1966: Memorial service at Utter-McKinley Wilshire Chapel, Los Angeles. Eulogy by Art Evans Sr.

August 27, 1971: Mollie Miles marries Paul Hinkley.

1973: Mollie Miles dies.

1984: Jaime, Peter and Patty's daughter, and Mollie and Ken's granddaughter is born.

2001: Ken Miles inducted into the Motorsports Hall of Fame, Sports Cars Category.

Mollie and Ken.   *Photo from the Art Evans Sr. estate*

Mollie Miles wrote an article titled, "Miles Away!" about her husband, which was printed in the November 1954 edition of *Road & Track* magazine. It is reprinted here with the kind permission of Editor Tom Bryant:

A recent newspaper report described Ken as a thin-faced, forty-four year old Englishman. Thin and English he undoubtedly is, but as yet is only 35 years old. He was born in Sutton Coldfield, England, in November 1918 at the house of his grandfather, a tea and coffee importer.

As a child, Ken's interests lay chiefly in taking his toys apart to see how and why they worked, which seems to be a fairly common trait in small boys, and in building complicated mechanical devices with his Meccano set. His early school days are veiled in a kindly mist, but there is a fairly general understanding that as a scholar, he was a dead loss, and to this day he is very frequently unable to decipher his own writing; he is, however, an avid reader and can carry on the most involved discussion on a remarkably diverse number of subjects.

At an early age, he developed a fascination for guns which led on one occasion to some very harsh words from a neighbour whose entire apple crop one year was ruined by marksmanship practice from Ken's rifle. Hurt by this man's lack of understanding, my husband retaliated one night when the neighbour was entertaining a group of Church dignitaries by swarming up a large tree which gave access to the neighbour's roof, and dropping a couple of dozen live frogs down the chimney into the open hearth beneath. This preoccupation with roof climbing led to another unfortunate episode some months later when Ken was exploring the roof of his grandpar-

ents' three-story house and by an error of judgment fell over the edge, clear through the glass roof of the patio in which his grandmother was at the time entertaining a knitting party. By great good luck, the Miles body was comparatively unharmed, but the knitting party was completely disorganized.

About eleven years old at this time, Ken's interests were beginning to be centered on motor bikes and cars, and great was his joy when a friend several years older acquired a 350 cc. Trials Special Triumph. Many happy hours were spent on illicit rides on this machine, culminating a couple of years later in a sad episode involving a dark night, a lamp post and a heap of stones left at the roadside by a careless gang of road menders. Injuries to the rider consisted mainly of a broken nose and the loss of three teeth, but the motorbike fared rather badly, and Ken had a hard time at the hands of the irate owner. Next the friend acquired a twin-cam 1100-cc Salmson which consistently shed its bearing and leaked oil into its water. After w awhile, these habits became rather too hard to take, so Ken and his friend finally figured out an ingenious solution. They wrapped shim brass carefully around the crankshaft until the connecting rods fitted, and then advertised the car for sale. An appointment was made to meet the prospective buyer on top of a hill, and when he hove into sight, Ken quickly poured in some water and started up the engine. The man drove smartly down the hill with no trouble at all, professed himself satisfied, parted with his money and drove away, at which time Miles and his friend left in the opposite direction for a short vacation, leaving no forwarding address. They never heard any more about the episode.

When he was fifteen years old, Ken was introduced by a friend to a couple of high school girls, and after the meeting said to one of them, "I'm going to marry that girl." To this end, he applied himself with such single mindedness that his headmaster finally phoned his parents to plead, "Can't you do something about this Mollie business?" His parents duly wasted much breath on this project, and Ken continued his wooing, working intermittently on the building of an Austin 7 Special named Nellie. This little car had a modified induction and exhaust system and a higher-than-standard compression ratio. On occasions, I would go along and polish it. (I was young and enthusiastic in those days.) I was even entrusted with the sacred task of painting it--British Racing Green, natch! The little car was a great success and was finally sold during the War. When last heard of, it was still going strong.

After he left school, aged sixteen, Ken was apprenticed to Wolseley Motors, where he slowly worked his way through every phase of automobile production from sweeping the floor upwards. For transport, he ran a Velocette motorbike, which he was forced to sell when he lost his driving license for a year through speeding. The sentence probably would not have been quite so heavy had he not made a gesture of derision at the pursuing cop, and when this was mentioned at the court, the presiding magistrate, an elderly spinster, asked the cop to state what the gesture in question had been. The officer, who was very young and very new to the Force, finally made a half-hearted and blushing attempt at indication, only to be completely annihilated when the Magistrate further probed, "I don't understand, Constable, what exactly does this mean?"

September 1939 found Ken within eight weeks of completing his apprenticesship, but on the day that the war started, he was in camp with the Territorial Army, and was immediately posted to an anti-aircraft unit located in the chief armament producing area of England. Here he saw plenty of excitement, but after about a year, he was posted to a driver-training regiment in Blackpool, where he struggled to teach unwilling soldiers how to drive Army vehicles; his worst headaches were the London taxi drivers, who were convinced that nobody would teach them anything. The only two high spots of his sojourn here were our marriage and the time his nose was broken in a terrific tavern brawl, by an ally armed with a broken bottle. This time the nose was broken in the opposite direction which evened things up.

Next came a transfer to the newly formed Royal Corps of Electrical and Mechanical Engineers, which involved a course in the south of England. Emerging from this with the highest marks of anyone on the course and the rank of staff sergeant, Ken was posted to a tank unit on the east coast. After several more postings throughout England and Scotland, during which the Miles proboscis was broken twice more, Ken joined the invasion of Europe on D-Day plus two. This gave him his first introduction to American food. Crossing a rough sea in a flat-bottomed invasion craft; they were offered bacon, sweet corn and syrup-- for breakfast, yet!

Ken saw service in Normandy, France, Holland, Belgium and Germany, working on tank reconnaissance and recovery, frequently a very gruesome job, and his was the first British unit to pass through the notorious concentration camp at Bergen-Belsen. When the war ended, he was stationed on the Baltic coast of Germany where he spent his off-duty time organizing motorcycle races and sailing yachts--and recalling prewar racing at Donnington Park where he had spent a lot of time studying the technique of the top drivers.

He was demobbed from the Army in January 1946 after nearly seven years' service, and bought a Frazer-Nash while I wasn't looking. This was the electron Nash, all light alloy, and after Kenneth had inserted a Ford V8 engine, it went like the proverbial bomb. He ran it with some success in hill climbs at Prescott and Shelsley Walsh and also in club events at the Silverstone circuit, and it was probably at this time that he began to be noticed as a driver.

He returned to Wolseley Motors where he was engaged for some time in tool making. However, there seemed little chance for advancement, and when asked to

join a friend in the production of race cars, the temptation was quite irresistible. The race car in question was a 500cc originally designed by Paul Emery with front-wheel drive and rubber cord suspension. The overall dry weight was 475 lbs. Ken loved every minute of this work, but it was very exacting, since it was necessary for him to spend about 100 hours a week on the project in order to carry out their order on schedule. After several months, the long hours and lack of sleep took quite a heavy toll on his health, and he lost 14 lbs. in weight besides getting very nervous and run down. Eventually he was forced to take a break, and about this time was offered a job with Gough Industries here in California. We had always wanted to visit America, so we decided to take the gamble and come--a move which we have never regretted.

Ken left England just before Christmas 1951 and took up his post as service manager at Gough's where he soon felt quite at home and happy. Soon, Ken began entering sports car races, running with a stock MGTD at first and later with a Mark II. Before long, he was working on the production of an MG Special. The design was entirely his own and apart from the engine, the car was composed solely of stock MG and Morris components. I shall never forget the Special's first appearance, which was at Pebble Beach 1953. There having been absolutely no opportunity to test the car previously, we had no idea what would happen in the race and were prepared for almost anything except what did take place. Even when Ken swung into the lead, our excitement was tempered with the thought that "there's many a slip," but when he hung on lap after lap, the suspense literally became almost unbearable as the end of the race approached.

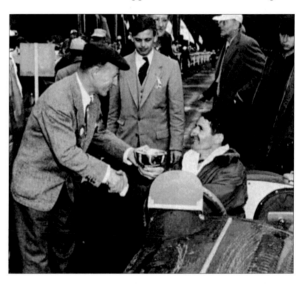

Right: Miles receiving the Pebble Beach Cup from Charles Christensen in 1953. *Photos from the Peter Miles collection.*

When it was all over and the race was won, we both were wondering the same thing, was it a flash in the pan, or would the car prove to be a real winner? We could hardly wait for the next race. Most of you know the little car's history from then on.

Now Ken is working on a new number 50, but due to the many demands on his very limited spare time, we have no idea when it will be making its first appearance. When it finally does, we shall undoubtedly die another thousand deaths. Let's hope it will be worth it!

The Wolseley Sheep-Shearing Machine Co. Ltd. was established in 1897 by Frederick York Wolseley. Bert Austin became manager in 1893 and Wolseley died in 1899. The first car was made in 1895. By WWI, Wolseley was one of the largest carmakers in England.

During the war, the company turned to military production. During the early twenties, the company was nearly bankrupt due to a strike. William Morris (Lord Nuffield) stepped in and bought the company for a fraction of its assets. Toward the end of the decade, Lord Nuffield introduced the Morris Minor, which became a mainstay of the company along with the Austin.

Schoolboy Ken Miles, at age 15, built an Austin 7 Special, which he was too young to race. His girlfriend, Mollie, painted it British Racing Green. Despite the fact he couldn't quality for a license, Ken drove it with great verve on lightly traveled English byways. Neither Mollie's nor Ken's reminiscences reveal if young Ken was ever apprehended by the reeve of the shire.

In 1934, Ken Miles dropped out of high school and became apprenticed to Wolseley Motors. Starting out as a janitor, by the start of WWII, Ken had worked his way up to fabricating and assembly.

When Miles started at Wolseley, the best-known model was the Hornet. These were fitted with various saloon (sedan) bodies on a lengthened Morris Minor frame.

Lord Nuffield had been operating Wolseley Motors as his own business, but in 1935, he transferred it to Morris Motors. Previously, Wolseley made engines for Morris.

The bottom photograph is of a 1937 Wolseley Super Six drophead (convertible) tourer. Production was interrupted when WWII started in September 1939. Ken Miles enlisted in the British Army that same month.

The company again converted to the production of military materiel. By 1942, 6,000 six-wheeled trucks had been produced. The factory was bombed 176 times between 1939 and 1945.

In January 1946, Miles was discharged and returned to Wolseley Motors as a toolmaker. Large parts of the factory had been destroyed by the Luftwaffe and the company had to decide how to return to civilian production.

In 1949, Wolseley was merged into British Leyland. In 1975, the name, Wolseley, was retired.

The photograph on the top of this page is of a 1934 Wolseley Hornet Special. Hornet chassis were sold to various coachbuilders who produced sports car versions. 1934 Hornets had a 1378cc six-cylinder engine. Later in the decade, some examples were fitted with 1604cc Wolseley Fourteen engines. Many Hornet Specials were raced and rallied against MGs and Rileys of the day.

While in the army, Staff Sergeant Ken Miles wrote a letter to the editor of the British magazine, *Motor Sport*. It was printed in the August 1943 edition:

Sir: Judging from several of the letters that have been written by my fellow readers to your most excellent journal, I imagine that few people in the country are familiar with the recent trend of American engine design. Don't get me wrong; I am a vintage enthusiast first and foremost, yet in my work I have to deal with a lot of American vehicles and the design of some of them shows great promise from a sporting point of view.

Look at this specification: 6-cylinder o.h.v. engine, bore 3 3/4 in., stroke 3 3/4 in., compression ratio 6.15 to 1. Hemispherical cylinder heads with inclined push rod operated valves. Die-cast pistons with domed semi-deflector heads to give a good combustion chamber shape. Short, stiff connecting rods with very large big-end bearings and fully floating pressure lubricated gudgeon pins. Camshaft machined all over, pressure lubricated bearings, driven by large fibre helical spur gear, also pressure lubricated. Inserted valve seats, and exhaust valve with a head of different metal from the

stem, the joint being fused just below the valve head. Valve timing: Inlet opens 28 degrees after b.d.c. Exhaust opens 76 degrees before b.d.c.; closed 45 degrees after t.d.c. 72 degrees of overlap.

Crankshaft a beautifully clean forging carried on very large main bearings. The clutch is a cunning device without springs or withdrawal arms, both of these being replaced by a heavy diaphragm which does both jobs.

When one considers that this is a trade engine and that the finish on it is really very good, and that the cooling systems and porting are both excellent, it would seem to be an engine possessing great possibilities as a post-war power plant. After the war a supercharged version is going into a four-wheel drive trials job of my own design, and we shall see what happens.

I am, Yours etc., K. H. Miles, S/Sgt.

After the war, Miles installed a supercharged Mercury V8 engine in his pre-war Frazer-Nash. He competed in hill climbs, trials and an occasional club race. His very first race was at Silverstone on April 23, 1949. He placed second in the over-3000cc class. His last race in England was on May 19, 1951, also at Silverstone. His finish was not listed in *Autosport*. The photographs on this page and the next one were taken by Guy Griffiths and are from the Jim Sitz collection.

The photo in the left-hand column was taken on June 12, 1949 during the Prescott Hill Climb. Ken placed 2nd in the over-3000cc class. The upper photo in this column was taken on April 23, 1949 at Silverstone. Again, Miles placed 2nd in class. The photo below was taken during another Prescott Hill Climb on May 22, 1949. This time he placed first in class with a time of 51.59 seconds. All were in his Frazer-Nash with a flat-head Mercury engine. The photo in the lower-left column was taken at the Great Auclum Hill Climb on July 23, 1950, where he placed second in a "Triangle Special." *All photos are by Guy Griffiths from the Jim Sitz collection.*

Ken Miles is sitting in his first MG Special, R-1. Standing behind him is Gough Industries employee Lorentz Mevold and General Manager John Beazley. *Photo by Bob Canaan from the John Beazley collection.*

John Beazley is the reason Ken Miles and his family immigrated to California. John and Ken came from the same town in England, Sutton Coldfield. Ken was somewhat older than John and even though they attended the same schools, they were not, as some reports would have it, childhood friends.

Ken's grandparents' house was a few doors from the Beazley home. The incident that involved the Miles' took place during the war. The Germans dropped an incendiary bomb setting the Miles home ablaze. John, and others in the neighborhood, helped put out the fire.

Both John and Ken were apprenticed to Wolseley Motors. After the war, Miles returned to Wolseley and the company sent Beazley to the states as their North American representative. Carroll Shelby remembers meeting John when he traveled to Texas.

One of the Wolseley accounts was Gough Industries, the MG and Morris distributor in Southern California. Beazley became acquainted with Phil Gough Sr. and was subsequently offered the job of general manager of the Gough Automotive Division, which John accepted.

The company was having problems in its service department, so John thought of Ken and the rest is history. Ken arrived in December 1951 and took over as service manager. Mollie and Peter followed to California shortly thereafter.

On April 20, 1952, Miles ran his first race in the U.S. at Pebble Beach in a Gough Industries MG-TD. During this first season in an absolutely stock MG, Miles' ability soon became apparent. At Stockton on August 24, he placed 9th overall in the under-1500cc main event. *Road & Track* dubbed the drive, "remarkable." At the December Torrey Pines, he came in 4th overall in the under-1500cc main event. Roger Barlow wrote that the feat was "tremendous."

During the year of campaigning the Gough TD, Ken began to work on an MG Special at the Gough facility. Although, according to Beazley, Ken did most of the work in his spare time, all of the components belonged to the company, as did the finished car. For publicity reasons, Beazley insisted that the car bear some resemblance to an MG. At the time, stock MGs were fitted with 1250cc engines. The engine in R-1 was a special 1500cc version supplied to Gough by the factory. The special engine and the MG-TC gearbox were disassembled and reassembled after each race.

For the most part, the construction as well as the maintenance was performed after hours and on weekends. Two Gough employees, Lorentz Melvold and Arne Bjorkli helped Ken. Melvold was a construction engineer. All three were paid for their work on R-1 as well as on R-2. Beazley made sure that they got time and a half.

When the TF came out, it was decided to build a second special that resembled the new model, hence the R-2. The same engine and gearbox were taken from R-1 and installed in R-2. Ken advertised R-1 and it was sold to Cy Yedor, who had been campaigning his own less successful MG Special.

In May 1955, Ken was fired as a result of a disagreement with the company controller. Phil Gough, Sr. gave him R-2 in lieu of severance pay.

BERNARD CAHIER REMEMBERS

I'm sitting here in Southern California with my friend, Art Evans, who has just turned on his tape recorder. We are remembering about our good friend, Ken Miles.

When Phil Hill and I were selling cars at Roger Barlow's International Motors in Hollywood in 1952, I went racing at Pebble Beach with my new MGTD. My wife, Joan, and I drove up the coast. When we arrived, we removed the bumpers, folded down the windscreen and went onto the track. That's when I first met Ken. He was also racing a TD. I really liked the guy. He was very English, a lot of fun, very warm. We became good friends.

Ken with the Gough Industries MGTD in 1952. *Photo: Peter Miles collection*

In 1953, Ken arrived on the scene with his new MG Special (R-1). Before that, Roger Barlow's Simca Specials were often the winning cars in the under-1500cc modified class. But from then on, Ken dominated it.

After that, I went back to Europe. When Ken got involved with Carroll Shelby and the Cobras, Miles became very important, not only because he was a wonderful driver, but also a great test driver. He was very technically minded. I think he was behind the development of a better Cobra as well as the GT40. By then, he was coming to

Europe all the time and I enjoyed seeing him. 1966 was a great year for Ford because, for the first time, they won Le Mans. It was a great photo finish and Ken was a part of it. What a great disappointment for him not to win after all he had done for Ford and Shelby.

Bernard Cahier, taken in October 2003 by Art Evans. After leaving Roger Barlow, Bernard became one of the most respected international motor racing photographers and journalists. For many years, he was the European correspondent for *Road & Track* magazine.

The following article was written by Ken Miles and appeared in the December 1953 edition of *Road & Track* and is reprinted here with the permission of Editor Tom Bryant.

KEN MILES' SPECIAL MG

By Ken Miles

An awful lot of nonsense has been written in the technical press about my MG, so for the benefit of anybody who may be interested, here is the story straight, as it were, from the horse's mouth.

In the middle of 1952 it became quite obvious to the writer that racing a stock MG or even a somewhat modified MG whilst enormous fun was, in fact, going no place at all, so in August work commenced on the drawing board for the construction of an MG special. The objective to be achieved was to build an MG fast enough to deal with the then supreme Simcas and Porsches within rigid limitations of cost, time and labor available. The motor car had to be as cheap as possible to build and had therefore to be constructed exclusively of readily obtainable stock component parts, and since it was to be built in a workshop, the most elaborate equipment was a welding outfit and an electric drill, the design had to be simple.

Bearing in mind the nature of the average American road race circuit, it was decided to build a motor car which had, above everything else, good acceleration out of a turn, was controllable on a bumpy surface and yet retained a reasonable degree of road holding ability in a fast open bend. Furthermore, it was decided to build a motor car into which any one of a number of engines could be fitted.

To achieve the desired results a layout was chosen which used a simple tubular chassis constructed of 3 1/2" O.D. by .063 wall thickness mild steel tube, the front suspension to be designed around the Morris Minor steering rack and torsion bars, and the rear suspension by quarter elliptic springs in order to concentrate the greatest suspension stress as near to the center of the chassis as possible. In the final design, the Morris Minor torsion bar ends were very close to the center cross member of the chassis so that the maximum suspension stresses are fairly evenly spread over the whole length of the frame. Considerable attention was given to achieving the maximum possible roll stiffness at the front of the motor car commensurate with good road holding and a minimum roll stiffness at the rear to diminish the tendency of the inside wheel to lift in a turn. Knock-off wheels were chosen in spite of the weight penalty involved because of the greatly enhanced brake drum cooling and the possibility of there being long distance races held in the future which may necessitate wheel changes. The front wheels were finally mounted on a combined T.C.-Series Y front hub running on a Series Y stub and swivel pin which was in turn mounted on A-frames of similar proportions to the MGTD, but fabricated from 1" O.D. by .063 wall thickness steel tube. The rear axle housing is MGTC with modified spring hangers to accommodate quarter elliptic springs below the axle and radius arms above the axle. The quarter elliptic springs locate the axle sideways and the short radius arms above the axle combined with the springs take the breaking and driving torque. The radius arms are rubber bushed at both ends to permit deflection of the axle abut the chassis center line, the front ends of the radius arms being mounted on a vertical extension, fabricated from a variety of sections of steel tube. This extension serves also as the mounting for the rear shock absorbers, and the rearward extension which supports the spare wheel and gas tank.

The original engine projected for this chassis was an MG TD engine equipped with a Laystall crankshaft, which reduced the stroke of 68.8 millimeters. This, with a standard block bored to plus .060" would have given a capacity of 998 c.c., the then prevailing maximum capacity for supercharged cars running in the 1 1/2 litre class. The object was to run a supercharged 1,000 c.c. engine at the maximum r.p.m. which the valve gear was capable of handling, some 7500 r.p.m., as the factory advised us that we could expect something in the region of 75 horsepower from such an engine. However, in the early part of 1953 we were advised by the factory that they could make available to us one of the small series of MG Mark II engines for which special cylinder blocks had been cast enabling a bore of 72 millimeters to be achieved, resulting in a capacity of 1466 c.c. Since the use of this engine would greatly reduce the weight of the car by eliminating the supercharger and supercharger drive and the power available promised to be about the same we stopped work on the supercharged engine, thus being able to concentrate our efforts on the chassis which was by now beginning to take shape.

The next problem which arose and one which had been causing the writer some considerable concern ever since the start of the construction, was what to do for a body. The obvious solution was a fiberglass shell, but after a study of the cost, particularly in time and labor, of constructing a fiberglass body, the idea was abandoned, time being particularly in short supply. The cost of a professionally constructed body is beyond all reason, so we decided to make an effort to clothe our chassis in the minimum quantity of aluminum which would constitute a body. Starting from an underpan the body was constructed by the fairly simple method of attaching the bottom edge of a sheet of aluminum to the motor car, bending it around the motor car by brute force and drilling holes in appropriate places for bolts to fasten it in position before we let go of it. The result, though not particularly handsome has one outstanding virtue, it cost us something less than $60.00

The nose piece presented a problem which appeared insoluble, and we eventually were forced to have this item constructed professionally, the labor cost alone eventually turning out to be greater than the total cost of the whole of the remainder for the body. Time did not permit the construction of a fancy radiator grille for the Pebble Beach race so a suitable portion was removed from the wire mesh screens which surround the Parts Department and inserted in the hole. Subsequently, a Morris Minor radiator grill was cut in half and turned endways filling the orifice more handsomely, this item being chrome plated and serving also to obscure from the vulgar gaze the internals of our cooling system.

Prior to Pebble Beach, the motor car had never run and we did not seriously expect it to survive practice. Much to our astonishment nothing broke during practice, and to our even greater astonishment nothing fell off during the race, and the only modification we have subsequently had to make to the motor car are slight alterations to the carburetor mounting and the addition of one extra leaf in each of the rear springs.

For the benefit of the many enquirers, the origin of the various parts not mentioned above is as follows: Engine, except for the block and detail modifications to the lubrication system and camshaft, the engine is a stock Mark II engine, retaining stock crankshaft, bearings, valves, valve springs, rockers, cam followers, etc. Gearbox: stock TD. Radiator: Morris Minor. Shock absorbers: Swanson Shock Absorber Service. Brakes: TC rear and Series Y front, the front modified to two leading shoes. Wheels: TC hub shells spoked to domestic 15" rims.

The dry weight of the car was estimated before construction commenced to be between 1200 and 1300 pounds. When we finally got the car to the scales, it turned out to have a dry weight of 1225 pounds.

Of the horsepower available, I can only say that it is more than such a conservative design should pretend to give, and not as much as we would like.

The estimated cost of construction of the car exclusive of direct labor costs, about $1,000, inclusive of labor would be somewhere in the region of $3,000, and if you ask me to build another for sale, I should ask $5,000.

The first outing for the new MG Special (R-1) was at Pebble Beach on April 19, 1953. Miles won first overall in the Pebble Beach Cup for cars under 1500cc. The 48-lap race was 100.8 miles long, an astonishing feat for an untested car. In doing so, Ken defeated Bill David in the hottest small car of the era, an Osca MT-4. Jackie Cooper was fifth in another MG Special. *Photo by Ralph Poole from the Ron Kellogg collection.*

Miles' 1953 season with the first MG Special, R-1, was an unprecedented success. He entered a total of 10 semi-main (under-1500cc) events and won every one! In those days, semi-main and main (over-1500cc) events were one-hour races. Usually, the main followed immediately after the semi. At seven of the 1953 meetings, Ken also ran in the main events and came in second overall three times and third two times. *This photograph was taken at the Long Beach MG Club staged Terminal Island event on October 4, 1953 by the late Dean Batchelor and is from the Ron Kellogg collection.*

On July 12, 1953, the one and only road race was held at Chino Airport. The event was conducted by the Four Cylinder Club of America. The club normally sponsored rallies; this was the one and only race for the organization.

Ken Miles won the under-1500cc semi-main event followed by John Von Neumann in his Porsche. The over-1500cc main event was won by Bill Stroppe in his Mercury-powered Kurtis. Miles came in second ahead of Howard Wheeler in a Ferrari and Von Neumann.

Stroppe prepared the factory-sponsored Lincolns that dominated the final years of the Mexican Road Race. Von Neumann went on to become the Western States distributor for Volkswagen and Porsche as well as Ferrari.

At early events, Ken was often more formally attired than the rest of us. *These photographs were taken by Dean Batchelor and are from the collection of Ron Kellogg.*

Ken and R-1 won the semi-main at Moffett Field on August 16, 1953. He went on to place third overall in the main event. In 1953, Ken had to travel far from Southern California to get in a full season of racing. When he became president of the Cal Club, he made sure there were 10 or 11 events every year. *Photo by Dean Batchelor from the Ron Kellogg collection*

JOE PLAYAN REMEMBERS

I met Ken Miles in 1953. Before that, Chick Leson from San Francisco had come to one of our Southern California events. While we were talking about Chick's new MG Special built by Hageman, the topic came up about some guy who was working at Gough Industries. He was from England and had been a tank driver in WWII. Nobody had ever heard about him before then.

Ken was always outspoken and sure of himself. When he came to the party at tech inspection with his new MG Special (R-1), he was asked if he was concerned about the cars with which he would be competing like the OSCAs of Bill David and Al Coppel as well as Chick's new MG Special. I didn't know Ken at the time, but I was taken by his quick response and cockiness. He said he was sure that the competition would be no trouble at all.

In Ken's first race with the MG Special (the 1953 Pebble Beach), he cleaned house. He was so fast that it was claimed the car couldn't be legal. At the time, I used to visit Ken at Gough Industries. Eventually, I bought Chick Leson's MG Special and installed a 1500cc engine I bought from Gough.

I was so impressed with Miles' driving and the rapidity of his car that I would visit him at Gough in order to try to get information about the car. He was always very gracious and helped me with different aspects of the new engine. We also talked about suspension and brakes. I was from the old school and believed that everything on the car had to be firm, even the tires. At the time, my mechanic was Lou Falcon, who used to race in the thirties. Suspension wise, everything was firm. Ken believed the opposite. Needless to say, Miles was right.

Ken Miles could drive just as fast in the rain as when the surface was dry. We all thought he must have had web feet. Racing against Ken was always a pleasure. He was a pro on the track. I remember one time at Santa Barbara when Ken was driving for John Von Neumann in a Porsche RS Spyder. I had a brand new RS Spyder and passed him for the very first time. After the race, Ken came over to my pit to find out what we had done to the engine to get so much speed. I introduced him to Lou Falcon

I really took to Ken; he was a maverick like myself.

Joe Playan leads Ken Miles at Pomona. Jack Nethercutt in his Lotus MK XI follows. *Photo by George Robitschek from the Joe Playan collection*

At the first SCCA National race in Southern California, held on November 8, 1953 at March Air Force Base, Ken Miles blew away the best the country had to offer in the under-1500cc event. Here he is passing Jim Simpson from Chicago in his Osca on the last lap. *Photo by Dean Batchelor from the Ron Kellogg collection.*

The first event of the1954 season was the Palm Springs Road Races held on January 23-24. The big surprise came on Saturday when Cy Yedor, driving Al Coppel's MG Special, succeeded in defeating Ken in R-1. Miles redeemed himself on Sunday, however. He won the semi-main, the Desert Trophy and came in third overall in the Palm Springs Cup, the main event for cars over 1500cc. The next event was at Bakersfield where Ken won not only the semi, but also the main event. After the April Pebble Beach, R-1 was sold to Cy Yedor. *Photo by Dean Batchelor from the Ron Kellogg collection.*

BILL POLLACK REMEMBERS

I'm not really sure when and where I first met Ken, but I remember seeing him at Gough Industries. He usually had grease smeared on his face and was busy building something. He would have a frame laid out or he was working on an engine. At that time, I was working for Petersen Publishing and Gough was one of my advertising accounts.

Ken lived up off of Pacific Drive at 2810 Sunday Trail in a really lovely setting. His house was on kind of a hillside with big trees around. His wife, Mollie, a total opposite from Ken, was a delightful person. Ken was pretty aggressive.

I found it difficult to understand him. He had a British accent that probably you would have needed to be a Brit to truly comprehend. It was hard for me to know what he was saying. Ken was very serious about racing. He knew what he wanted to do and how to do it.

As I recall, he was a very good administrator. He got involved with the Cal Club, got on the board and was president three times. He did a lot of good things for the club. He had lots of good ideas.

By the time I got to know Ken, I was already driving the large-displacement modified cars. Ken usually drove in the under-1500cc group and we didn't have that much of an opportunity to fraternize.

Ken stood out. He was fast right from the beginning and got everybody's attention. It looked as if he was driving the wheels off cars. I was always very impressed with the way he went. Even though Ken usually drove in an under-1500cc car, he was usually also in the main event with the over-1500cc machines. When you are out on the track, you automatically get an idea whether or not this guy is safe in terms of getting around. With a lot of drivers, you tend to give them plenty of room and wait until you have a clear shot to pass.

With Ken, I never had any qualms about what he was going to do. I always knew he was going to do it right. He never did something dumb. I had a lot of respect for him.

We weren't really close as friends. We didn't have a lot in common other than cars and racing. I remember him as a good family man; his son, Peter, was delightful. Peter was very much like his mother. He resembled Mollie more than Ken.

Ken probably did more to sell MGs than anyone else during that era. He was a consummate salesman for the marque. It's interesting that his two MG Specials are around today in vintage. But they don't go the way they did when Ken had them. The difference is the right foot. He would just go farther into a corner and he had a better feel for what a car was capable of doing; he would go right out to the very edge. Even today—professionals an exception, of course—there are not a lot of people who can drive like that, particularly at the club level like we were then. In those days, there were only a handful who could drive like that. Most club racers then drove with some restraint; with Ken, it was all out.

Ken in the Troutman-Barnes Special leading Bill Pollack in the Baldwin Special at the 1954 Golden Gate. *Photo: Jim Pollack*

CY YEDOR REMEMBERS

In 1954, I bought Al Coppel's MGTC Special and was driving it at Pebble Beach. Ken was driving his first MG Special, R-1. After a previously undefeated season, Ken's MG engine gave up the ghost while he was in the lead and he was back in the paddock. I was having a lot of trouble with Al's MG. The car lost the clutch and the radiator was boiling over and spraying hot water in my face. After four or five laps, I decided to quit.

When I pulled into the pits, Miles was standing there. He walked over and asked me, "What's wrong, bloke?" I said nothing except the clutch is out; it's overheating and steaming in my face. I've had enough." Ken said, "How about letting me drive the bloody thing." I said, "Sure, get in," and out he went. He finished in third place! After the race, he told me, "Don't ever drive that bloody dangerous thing again. That's the worse car I've ever been in. I'll tell you what I'm going to do. I'm building a new MG special and I'll sell you the old one so you'll have something decent."

That's how I got R-1. I don't remember how much I paid, but I was more than happy with the car and did rather well with it. What I got was a roller or perhaps with a junker engine. I had Bud Hand build me an engine. It was good, but not as good as the special factory engine that was in it when Ken drove it. Even though it wasn't as quick with the Hand engine, I had good luck with the car.

I used to have a machine shop in Vernon. We worked from 7 a.m. till 3 p.m. On my way home, I used to come up Alameda Street and stop at Gough Industries. I watched him build R-2. We got to be very good friends.

During the rest of 1954, Ken drove a variety of cars while R-2 was being built. The first race of 1955 was at Willow Springs where Miles said, "The car ran like a sewer." Next on the calendar was March 26 and 27 at Palm Springs. On Saturday, the new Shingle was disqualified and I won. Somebody claimed there was some sort of a fender problem. Later in the day, Ken got it straightened out and won the consolation race.

On Sunday, we were both in the under-1500cc main event. At the start, Ken jumped into the lead with me following. After about half the race, he had stretched his lead to a half a lap. At Palm Springs there were two straights, the start-finish straight and the back straight. From one straight, we could see the cars on the other. I was on the back straight and noticed Ken on the start-finish straight gesturing for me to speed up. He slowed down and finally I caught up. We decided to put on a show and for the rest of the race, we diced nose to tail. Later I heard the announcer and the crowd were going crazy. As we entered the start-finish straight on the last lap, Ken's engine coughed and I surged ahead. Good Lord, I was going to win! So I backed off and let him pass. By the way, that was James Dean's first race and he came in third in his production Porsche Speedster.

Ken was just a wonderful guy to be around. And he was very open about everything he did. He always wanted to help others. What I remember most about Ken is that it was a pleasure to know him and he was a great friend. Knowing him was the high point of my racing life. He was a memorable guy and a standout. I don't know why they don't have him in the Automobile Hall of Fame. I've written letters, but nobody has ever even responded. This photo is the only one I have of us together.

Ken Miles in the rain driving the "Shingle" at the April 17, 1955 Pebble Beach. Ken won the semi-main event for cars under 1500cc and went on to place third in the main event. *Photo by Ralph Poole from the Ron Kellogg collection.*

Cy Yedor purchased R-1 from Ken. Cy went on to campaign the car very successfully. Yedor started racing in 1952 in his father's XK120 at Palm Sprngs. (Dad didn't know about it.) Through 1956, he competed in more than 50 races, winning six main events.

Ken Miles in R-2 (left) and Cy Yedor in R-1 chatting about this and that before the start of the 1955 Pebble Beach Cup race for modified cars under 1500cc. *Photo by Don Meacham from the Cy Yedor collection*

At the start of the 1955 Pebble Beach Cup, Ken took the lead and was never challenged. The field was made up of some very respectable iron. There were four Oscas, the fastest under-1500cc cars of the time with the exception of the Miles specials. In addition, there were John Von Neumann in a Porsche 550 Spyder and Pete Lovely in a VW-Porsche Special.

Behind Miles, a battle developed among Lovely, Von Neumann, Cy Yedor in R-1 and Harry Hanford in a Lotus-MG. Lovely and Von Neumann dropped out due to mechanical troubles and Hanford slowed, probably due to the rain. Chick Leson came up and dueled with Yedor for second place, finally passing to take the checkered flag in second place. Yedor was third.

The Miles win was not only a demonstration of his unsurpassed talent in constructing a race car, but also of his superior skill at driving in the rain. The celebrity of Pebble Beach brought Miles additional international attention.

Starting with the 1990 Monterey Historic Races, Cy presents a lithographed copy of the Eberts painting to the driver of an under-1500cc car who best represents the spirit of vintage racing.

A drenched Miles in the paddock at Pebble Beach. *Photo by Julian Graham*

This is a reproduction of a painting by Ken Eberts. The original is an 11x14 watercolor. It depicts Ken Miles in his famous MG Special R-2, "The Shingle," followed by Cy Yedor in Ken's first MG Special, R-1, at the Sixth Annual Pebble Beach Sports Car Road Race. The event took place on April 17, 1955 in the rain. The race was "The Pebble Beach Cup, Modified Division for Cars Under 1500cc." The distance was 48 laps; a little over 100 miles. Ken Miles won first overall followed by Chick Leson in an Osca MT-4. Cy Yedor was third. The others that made up the first ten finishers are notable: 4th - Harry Hanford in his Lotus MG, 5th - Al Coppel in an Osca Mille Miglia, 6th - Kjell Qvale in his MG Special, 7th - I. W. Stephenson in another MT-4, 8th - Joe Playan in his MG Special, 9th - Major Skip Swartly in an Osca Special and 10th - Jim Orr in the Devin-Panhard. Orr won the SCCA National Championship in the Devin. Swartly's engine was 1100cc, so he won Class G while Jim Orr won H. The original and prints are in color. This reproduction is printed here courtesy of Cy Yedor and Ken Eberts. One of my prized possessions is a print, autographed by Cy, which hangs over my fireplace. This black and white reproduction does not do justice to it.

AL MOSS REMEMBERS

My first encounter with Ken Miles was at the second Torrey Pines race in 1952. Ken was the service manager for Gough Industries, the MG importer, and he had entered an Mk II MGTD. He had removed most of the interior upholstery panels, which was verboten in the production classes. It was my duty, as tech inspector, to inform Ken that this was not allowed. Naturally, an argument ensued. "What difference does it make?" he asked. "If it doesn't make any difference, why did you remove everything?" I replied. He reinstalled everything and we became good friends.

A year or so later, Ken authorized my repair shop as one of the first MG Service Dealers. This meant I could purchase parts at the dealer price, do warranty work and receive all service bulletins. Ken would take me into the secret, private room at Gough where the two Scandinavian craftsmen, along with Ken, were constructing the first Miles MG Special, R-1.

I had the rare privilege of working with Ken on his pit crew for about nine months. Gordon Whitbey was the mechanic and I was in charge of lap scoring, timing and signaling. Once Ken was on the track, I had control of the car. I gave him a signal every lap. I can close my eyes and still see Ken coming by, usually at full speed, with his beak pointed straight ahead. As he passed, he would swivel his head 90 degrees to read my board.

Ken receiving congratulations for a win at Santa Barbara. Mollie Miles (with sun glasses) is second from the right. Mollie was almost always on hand to help Ken celebrate a win or commiserate for a loss. The man with a cowboy hat wearing a checkered shirt and holding Ken's right leg is mechanic Rolf Weutherich. Rolf was riding with James Dean when Dean was killed on September 30, 1955.
Photo from the Sports Car Journal archives

One time at Palm Springs, Ken was well placed in the main event. The next car to pass was a Jaguar special. I could see the car tank was coming adrift on the Jag, so I signaled to hold steady rather than passing. A lap or so later, the Jag was black-flagged. Ken trusted me and when I signaled, he would comply.

At the one and only race held at the Chino Airport, Ken won the under-1500cc semi-main and was running third in the main event. He was as far up as I thought he was capable, so I had him on "hold your position." For several laps, he came by pointing to the front of his car. I couldn't figure out what was wrong, so I got out the binoculars. Finally I decided he wanted to pass the car in front. I didn't know if he could, but nevertheless, next time around, I signaled, "speed up." Wham! He went right around and ended up taking second overall behind Bill Storppe in the Kurtis. I realized he was really following my instructions. If he was leading a race and I told him to come in, he would. If it turned out to be a false alarm, he would have killed me!

After my season with Ken, I became a race official: the chief race judge. At one Paramount Ranch, because of the narrow main straightaway and pit area, a rule was made that anyone wanting to make a stop had to use a new lane leading from the last turn into the pits. Ken was leading by a large margin when I heard over the communication line that he had stopped on the main straight while his mechanic came to hand him a cup of water. When he drove off, he tossed out the paper cup in Turn One. My judge at the start-finish wanted him disqualified, but Race Chairman Joe Weissman countermanded our ruling. The judge wanted to quit on the spot, but I told him we would sort it out later. Ken finished first. Afterward, all of the judges got together and voted unanimously to disqualify Ken. We submitted our ruling and it was upheld. Ken won the battle, but we won the war. The matter was discussed at the next board meeting. Ken was not only a member of the contest board, he was also the club president. He just laughed it off; it was no big deal for him. He never held it against me.

At Santa Barbara, I was always out on Turns 6, 7 and 8. They were slow and I could almost talk to the drivers. One time I was eating a sandwich. Ken saw me, so he stopped and I gave him half. In those days, things hung rather loose. If you even thought of doing something like that today, all the whistles would blow like mad.

At the 1953 Santa Barbara, I was crewing for Ken. He won. When he stopped, Ken's wife, Mollie, and his son, Peter, were hurrying over to congratulate him. Peter ran towards the car and I tried to get my blackboard between Peter and the hot exhaust pipe. Unfortunately, I was not successful and Peter was burned rather badly. Years later, I told Peter about the incident. He replied that he had always wondered how he got those scars on his leg.

Several years ago, Peter and his wife, Patty, stayed a night at my home in Santa Barbara. Next morning when they came to breakfast, I noticed Peter looked rather bleary eyed. It turned out he had stayed up all night looking through my library for information about his dad. I showed him a book that revealed why Ken didn't win the 1966 Le Mans. Peter had never heard the true story.

The season I spent crewing for Ken was a high point in my life. I have a lot of fond memories of Ken. In 1991 at the Monterey Historics I got to drive R-1. While I didn't attempt anything heroic, it was quite an emotional experience to be in Ken's car with so many others with which it competed during the fabulous fifties.

Al Moss in 1998.

1953 was the year Al Moss crewed for Miles. Ken won every single under-1500cc semi main event he entered as well as the first two in 1954. After the third race—the April Pebble Beach—R-1 was sold to Cy Yedor and Ken was building R-2. As it turned out, R-2 wasn't ready until 1955.

For the rest of 1954, Ken campaigned a variety of cars. He ran a newly introduced MGTF for Gough Industries with mixed results. Construction partners Dick Troutman and Tom Barnes had built a rather potent special. For the first time since he left England, Miles was at the wheel of an over-1500cc car. The prevailing wisdom at the time was that he was a small-car specialist and wouldn't or couldn't do well in cars in the larger modified class.

An MGA was entered in the F-Production Class by Phil Gough, scion of the Gough Industries family that distributed BMC cars.

The "Le Mans" start (drivers run across the track) of the six-hour enduro. *Photos by Harold Treichler from the Sports Car Journal archives*

The City of San Diego announced that the October 1955 event at Torrey Pines was to be the last before the start of the golf course development project. The article in the January 1956 issue of *Road & Track* was titled, "The last days of TORREY PINES." As it turned out, however, there was to be one more early the following year, after which the closure became final.

On Saturday, October 22, after practice, there was a six-hour endurance race. Ken Miles and his friend, Cy Yedor, drove the Gough Industries entry, a stock MGA. When the checkered flag fell, Ken and Cy were scored 18th overall and 4th in class. Ed Barker and Bob Drake in a Porsche Speedster won the class. Richie Ginther and Erich Buckler in another Speedster were 5 seconds behind. Jim Parkinson and Bobby Brigham in another Gough MGA were 5 seconds in front of Miles and Yedor.

The enduro was won by Pete Woods in his C-Type Jaguar. Second, more than one lap behind, were Phil Hill and Paul O'Shea in a production Mercedes-Benz 300SL.

Sunday saw the usual bill of fare: under 1500cc and over 1500cc production and modified plus a ladies. Ken won the under-modified race in front of a very respectable field that included the Porsche Spyders and an Osca MT-4. The Spyders were driven by top pilots Jean Pierre Kunstle, Jack McAfee and Johnny Porter. The author of this book, who had arrived too late to practice, finished 14th overall. Ugh!

As luck would have it, I had committed my car to be displayed in a car show at the Los Angeles Pan Pacific Auditorium. The show ended at 10 p.m. Saturday night. As soon as I could, I threw my sleeping bag and helmet into the car and drove—sans muffler—to Torrey Pines, 100 miles away. I slept through the morning practice and asked the chairman if I could start at the end of the grid. As the starting grid was determined by drawing numbers from a hat, my request was refused. As I had never before raced at Torrey Pines or even been around for a tour, I asked the guy in the car next to me, one Kenneth Miles, for his advice. He told me, "At the start, get the hell out of the way and then keep to the right and watch your mirror all the time." I followed his advice and lived to write about it.

DICK VAN LAANEN REMEMBERS

When Ken was the president of the California Sports Car Club, I was a board member. Together, he and I laid out the basic race courses at Pomona, Paramount Ranch and Bakersfield.

During that time, Ken was working for John von Neumann (the Western States distributor of Porsche and VW). At Pomona, we used one of the first Porsche Carreras. It had dual-overhead cams. I think it was the only one in the U.S. at the time. The car was so completely out of tune that it popped and snorted. It wasn't much fun for Ken.

Ken and I worked on laying out the course clockwise because this is the direction they use in Europe, unlike circle-track racing in the U.S. It seemed to work okay. But one time the stock car people had a race at Pomona and they ran it counterclockwise and it seemed to be better. So we turned ours around after our second race.

Ken and I both signed the contract on behalf of the Cal Club with the Pomona Elks Club. The venue was very successful. The races there provided the club with a lot of funds. I was the race chairman at the first event. We had a perfect day and great attendance.

I remember when we laid out the course at Paramount Ranch. We drove out to Agoura Hills in a Competition Motors (von Neumann's company) VW. Riding with Ken Miles was something else. We drove through the bushes and dirt to find out what would be the best layout. When we came back to Los Angeles, we went to Ken's home on Sunday Trail in the Hollywood Hills. The route to his house was narrow with wet streets and blind corners. Ken never heard of "moderation."

In 1954, we scheduled a race just north of Bakersfield at Minter Field, a general aviation airport. We had previously designed the layout, but a week before the event, Ken and I had to go and re-engineer the course. Our original design used all of the runways. In the meantime the airport management, however, decided that we had to leave one runway open for aircraft. On the Sunday morning the week before, we flew up in a DC3 and landed at Bakersfield Airport, a few miles south of our venue. Our race coordinator, Al Papp met us there. While I was driving Al's Porsche Speedster to plan the new layout, I noticed a DC3 overhead flying south. I called to Ken, "That's our airplane." He jumped in the passenger seat of Al's Porsche and we headed south to the Bakersfield Airport. Ken was beat-ing on the side of the car yelling, "Faster, faster." We got to the airport with 20 seconds to spare.

My experiences with Ken were all good. We never had any disagreements. I found both Ken and Mollie to be very gentle and understanding people. For me, he was a nice person to be around. I can't say it was thrilling to ride with him. It was kind of scary, really. But he never had an accident (on the highway) that I know of. It was an honor to have known him and to have worked with him.

Race Chairman Dick Van Laanen congratulates Ken on another win.

29

Ken Miles and John Lockett in MGA EX 182, Number 41, finished the 1955 24-Hours of Le Mans in twelfth place overall and fifth in class. The factory entered Ken because by then his exploits with MGs in the U.S. had received world-wide attention. This trip was the first time Miles had returned to Europe since he immigrated in 1951. He took the opportunity to visit his parents in England. *Photos by Bernard Cahier, courtesy Road & Track*

Miles in the "Shingle" at the October 1955 Torrey Pines. Dr. Paul Winters is in car 45, a Halliday Renault Special. Passing him is Jean Pierre Kunstle in W. R. Turner's battered 550 Porsche Spyder. Miles passed both and won the under-1500cc semi-main event. *Photo by Harold Treichler from the Sports Car Journal*

On December 3-4, 1955, the California Sports Car Club staged a race at Palm Springs. It was the ninth running at this venerable venue. As a matter of fact, the very first road races held in Southern California after WWII were there on April 16, 1950.

The event was significant for a number of reasons. Very occasionally, the gods of rain see fit to favor Palm Springs. December 3, 1955 was one such occasion. Most of the spectators went home and, even though it didn't rain on Sunday, they didn't return. This was unusual for Palm Springs, one of the most popular venues of the fifties. The previous running had seen some 22,000 spectators watch Ken Miles in his "Shingle" win the under-1500cc race while Jack McAfee took the main in a 4.5 Ferrari.

While Ken brought his "Shingle" to this December 1955 meeting, he didn't race it. Wealthy sportsman Tony Parravano had acquired a new 4-cylinder 1500cc Maserati. The car was so new that Tony had not entered in time for its inclusion in the program. There wasn't even time to paint proper numbers. As the photograph shows, the numbers appear to have been made of white masking tape.

Tony wanted his new car to win, so he prevailed on the best driver to chauffeur it: Ken Miles, obviously. Not wanting the "Shingle" to remain idle, Ken gave Harry Hanford the ride. This was one of the few times a car with the number 50 didn't have Miles at the wheel. Harry was among the top fifties-era small-car drivers. Nevertheless, proving cars aren't everything, Harry couldn't win.

In Saturday's under-1500cc semi-main, Ken won in the Maser, followed by Jean Pierre Kunstle in a 550 Porsche Spyder and in third, Hanford. Miles repeated on Sunday, this time with Johnny Porter in a Spyder second and, again, Hanford. Kunstle came in fourth.

In those days, it was often the practice to invite the first three cars in the under-1500 to compete in the main event, ostensibly for over 1500cc modified cars. On this occasion, Ken was the only one of the three who accepted. Both main events each lasted one hour in those days. Driving a race car for an hour can be both mentally and physically tiring. Miles, however, was always in top condition. He was slim, didn't smoke or drink much and worked out daily.

By the middle of the decade, Southern California sports car racing was getting increased national attention. Masten Gregory, a young

In a gab session with Masten sitting on his right. *Photo: Sports Car Journal*

man from Kansas, who had, some said, more money than sense, had taken notice of Palm Springs. (Asked how to make a small fortune in sports car racing, Briggs Cunningham answered, "Start out with a large one.") Gregory drove a 3-liter Maserati.

On that Sunday in Palm Springs, he defeated the best the Cal Club had to offer. Ernie McAfee ended up second by a few inches in the Bill Doheny Ferrari Monza. Chuck Daigh, who would later go on to greater glory in Lance Reventlow's Scarab, was third in the Troutman-Barnes Special. Miles in the little Maserati placed seventh overall and first in class. Among the cars behind him were two C-Type Jaguars, a Kurtis and a J2X Allard.

Ken Miles in Tony Parravano's 150S Maserati. *Photo: Sports Car Journal*

Miles' association with Tony Parravano didn't last long. The first event with the team was at Santa Barbara on September 3-4, 1955. Ken drove Tony's 4.9 Ferrari 375.

On Saturday, Ken drove the MG Special, R-2, to second place behind John Von Neumann in a Porsche Spyder. Then he jumped into the Ferrari and placed third behind Ernie McAfee and Phil Hill. On Sunday, he succeeded in defeating Von Neumann in the semi, but failed to finish in the Ferrari.

In March of 1955, Miles and Gough Industries came to a parting of the way. Ken went to work for Clem Atwater, who had a dealership in the San Fernando Valley.

Tony Parravano with Ken in the Ferrari. *Photo: Lester Nehamkin*

MILES SELLS MG, WILL DRIVE PORSCHE, FERRARI

It used to be Mr. MG.—but now it's Herr Porsche!

As predicted exclusively in the last issue of MOTORACING, Ken Miles, the famed English driver who was the No. 1 1500cc pilot on the Coast for 1955, will tool a Porsche Spyder in 1956.

And not only that—in the big-car category he will be driving Ferraris and Maseratis!

Miles was signed up as field representative by Johnny von Neumann, Porsche-Volkswagen dstributor. He will work on dealer-distributor relations under Regional Manager Sam Weill.

PORSCHE FIRST

The driver's other arrangement is with Tony Parravano, wealthy Inglewood contractor and owner of a string of Italian racers. Although not in Parravano's employ, Miles will drive for him. His first obligation, however, will be to von Neumann, which means the Porsche.

Ken won the under-1500cc feature in Parravano's 1.5-liter Maserati at Palm Springs recently. He had driven a 4.9 Ferrari for the Italian before.

DEBUT AT TORREY

Long a familiar figure (and winner) behind the wheel of his green MG Special, Miles last week sold the Shingle to Frank L. Lederer, a naval officer from San Francisco, who will commission Jack Duncan, Stockton, a Healey 100S driver, to pilot it.

Miles will debut under the dual banner at Torrey Pines Jan. 14-15.

Date Extended for New CSCC Licenses

Expiration date for issuance of new competition licenses for CSCC drivers has been extended from Dec. 31 to Jan. 31, it has been announced by the club's Contest Board.

Licenses are issued on basis of a written examination. Tests must be taken at the Club offices, 4949 Hollywood Blvd. Day hours are 9 to 5, Monday through Friday; evenings, 7:30 to 10, Thursday, Jan. 5; Thursday, Jan. 19; Thursday, Jan. 26; and Monday, Jan. 30.

The December 30, 1955 edition of *MotoRacing* reported that Ken Miles had gone to work for John Von Neumann's Competition Motors and would drive a Porsche Spyder for John.

The first race of the 1956 season was held on January 14-15 at Torrey Pines. Hard on the coast just north of San Diego, Torrey Pines was one of the most revered road courses in the U.S. during the early fifties. San Diego, however, had a different plan for the former Army

base. (Where John von Neumann took basic training after joining the Army at the start of WWII.) The city had announced that two golf courses would be built and that the October 1955 race would be the last for the venue. Construction hadn't started by the beginning of 1956, so one last event was held.

Action started with practice on Saturday morning. Miles, in his first time in a Porsche, managed to flip the car on the last turn. The Spyder was totaled. To put it mildly, John and Eleanor Von Neumann were not amused.

Photo from the Sports Car Journal archives

MotoRacing thought that Ken would also drive for Tony Parravano, but that was not to be. Parravano ended up having young Masten Gregory drive his Maserati 300S. This turned out to be a wise choice; Gregory won Sunday's main event against stiff competition.

Miles, fortunately, was uninjured in the accident. Porsche distributor Von Neumann just happened to have more than one 550. A stellar field lined up for the start of the Sunday under-1500cc main.

The group included five 550 Spyders and two Lotuses plus the famous "Pooper," Pete Lovely's Cooper with a Porsche engine. In addition to Ken and Lovely, among other drivers were Jack McAfee, John Porter, John Timanus and Tony Setember. Miles won by 16 seconds over Lovely who, it turned out, was never a real threat.

John Von Neumann congratulates Ken on his under-1500cc semi-main win. Standing between them is Eleanor Von Neumann. *Photos on this page from the Sports Car Journal archives.*

According to the April 1956 edition of *Road & Track*, "A crowd of 35,000 spectators who willingly braved the familiar coastal overcast to view what must have been the most notable entry list of cars and drivers ever to race at the Pines."

On Saturday, the 6-Hour event was won by Jerry Austin in a D-Type Jaguar. Three other Ds were driven by Sherwood Johnston, Pete Woods and Ignacio Lozano.

As the winner of Sunday's semi-main, Miles was added to the main-event field. Ahead of him on the starting grid were Phil Hill, Ernie McAfee, Masten Gregory and Sherwood Johnston among others. Stirling Moss was there too, but he ended up sitting it out due to the lack of an FIA sanction.

Al Torres flags off the main event. Behind Al is Ernie McAfee, Ferrari 121 LM, with Phil Hill in a Monza behind. Gregory is on the pole with Sherwood Johnston in the D-Type Jaguar behind Masten. Miles started dead last.

Miles, passing car after car, finished third overall behind Gregory and Ernie McAfee. Behind Ken were the Johnston D-Type, Chuck Daigh in the Troutman-Barnes plus Allards, Jaguars and 550 Spyders.

4 PROBLEMS BALK PRO RACING IN U.S. -- MILES

(These views on pro sports-car racing are those of Mr. Miles and do not express the opinion of MOTORACING.— Ed. Note.)

By Ken Miles
Noted British Driver and No. 1 West Coast Under-1500cc Winner in 1955

MANY OF OUR local sports writers are currently beating the drum for "professional sports car racing," and I feel that the people most likely to be affected, the sports car club members, should hear the other side of the argument.

I have raced under the European system in which no distinction is made between the amateur or professional driver and I know the advantages and weaknesses of this system. I have lived in America long enough to know why the European system will not work out here yet.

Roughly speaking, the problem is a fourfold one, comprised of — sanctioning, the SCCA, courses and drivers.

Taking sanctioning first, in Europe there exists an omnipotent body in the FIA, represented in each country by a national club, without whose sanction nobody can either promote a race or compete in one. Since the first concern of the FIA is "Will it be a good race from the sporting viewpoint?" And they are not in the least bit concerned whether the promoting club

KEN MILES
. . . Not Ready for Pros—Yet . . .

makes money or not—they can enforce regulations regardless.

PROFITS TO CHARITY

In Europe, the first question asked about a race is "Was it a good race?", and many of the largest races are supported by

(Continued on Page 10, Col. 3)

Continued from far right:

Sorry, the only copy of *MotoRacing* is damaged. Miles is saying that pro racing would be only to the tax advantage of main-event front runners.

la... ...oney. I... ...
money w... ...worth while and if the tax write off were practical, then the Parravanos, the Dohenys and Edgars would really make an effort to win, and the wealthy owners with the latest equipment and the highest salaried driver would reign supreme to the eventual exclusion of the ordinary club members.

Pro Racing Must Wait, Says Miles

(Continued from Page 1)
the large newspapers who assume complete financial responsibility, whilst turning over the entire control of the race to the organizing club and any profits to charity.

In this country, there is as yet no organization that can lay down the law and enforce it, and the get-rich-quick-promoter is only too quick to take advantage of this fact. The first question is "How much money did they make?"

Fortunately, the FIA is currently turning a blind eye to the activities of American drivers in races sponsored in America by a recognized club. If they recognize a national sanctioned body in America which, unlike AAA, will take an active interest in sports car racing, then this happy state of affairs must inevitably change, and drivers wishing to race outside the USA will race in FIA sanctioned races only — or not at all.

CAN'T PAY MONEY

Secondly, we have the problem of the SCCA. No sports car club is going to encourage its members to do something which will result in their being barred from such SCCA events as Pebble Beach. Because of the way most of the SCCA races are set up, a charity being the recipient of all the profits in exchange for their influence in helping to obtain the use of the course, the SCCA is certainly not in a position to pay prize money.

And what of the Los Angeles Region of the SCCA, which has consistently suffered financial catastrophe with its races? Will it go along with the proposal to pay prize money?

There would have to be a change of policy by the SCCA, which is extremely unlikely, or recognize the authority of some American National sanctioning body, such as USAC. After all, in America the SCCA and CSCC promote at the present all the sports car road races with the exception of Sebring, which is run under direct FIA sanction.

FIA IS STRICT

A driver who takes part in a race sponsored by some other body could find himself in a position where he could not race with the American sports car clubs, neither could he run in any other race in the world, since the FIA is extremely strict about drivers competing in races not sanctioned by itself. We have heard a great deal about the clubs being now in a position to afford to pay prize money. Are they?

This past year the CSCC made a nice little profit on the management, good luck with the weather, magnificent support from its members and satisfactory contracts with the various local entities, but its current bank balance would be rapidly converted to a deficit by two unlucky races. Furthermore, without a sufficient bank balance to finance the races the club would be forced to approach the small-time promoter, such as Bill White or George Cary, for sponsorship, with the net result that the club members would be working for free to line the pockets of the promoter.

Another major problem is the shortage of courses. In this country we depend too much on the good offices of the various civic bodies for the use of the courses on which we race. If the club is to pay prize money, it cannot at the same time turn over a large share of the profits to the civic bodies, and would be unable to...

We know from practical experience that a course is only good for two major events of one type a year, and with real estate at its present high price, few people will make the investment required to pave a permanent course for the return they can expect. Yet we need permanent low cost installation so that we can stage low-cost club events for our club members.

How would the drivers be affected? In order to be able to guarantee prize money, the promoter must guarantee a good gate, so he will tend to concentrate on the type of event which has the greatest spectator appeal. The weekend of racing, with 10 or 15 races for every type of car spread over Saturday and Sunday, with over 200 club members competing, would have to go, and would be replaced by one or two very short races, "curtain raisers," followed by one feature event.

Since most of our courses are, strictly speaking, safe for only about 25 cars at a time, some 100 club members would be deprived of a chance to race.

The crowd loves a "Big Name," and to draw the crowds the big name would always have priority of entry, whilst the others would be lucky if their entry was accepted for more than one race a year, just to make up the numbers.

STOCK PILOTS OUT

The stock MG driver, the stock Jag driver and the small sedan owners who complain even now of not getting enough racing would be out.

To attract the big names, most of the prize money would go to the first three places in the feature event, the others having to...

The May 19-20, 1956 event at Bakersfield was a banner one for both Miles and the Von Neumann Porsche Spyder. Ken won the semi-main event for cars under 1500cc on both Saturday and Sunday. This was the first time Miles won on both days for Von Neumann. *Photo from the Sports Car Journal archive.*

From the March 23-30, 1956 edition of *MotoRacing*

SCCA Mum on Petition Leading To Miles Membership Reject

By Gus V. Vignolle

KEN MILES, the noted British driver who was the leading under-1500cc winner in 1955 and long a militant foe of the Los Angeles Region of the Sports Car Club of America, has been given a neat harpoon right smack between the shoulder blades by both the local chapter and the National body.

No Little Lord Fauntleroy by any stretch of the imagination, Miles, past president of the California Sports Car Club, was suspended for six months by the local region for "discourteous and unsportsmanlike" conduct.

Then his application for membership was rejected by the National body after an all-out drive spearheaded here by a bitter foe, Duane Alan, activities chairman.

Miles had resigned from the SCCA after he refused to "submit to their ridiculous driver's
(Continued on Page 4, Cols. 1-2)

(Continued from Page 1)

test" some time ago. (In 1952, Alberto Ascari, then the world's champion, refused to take a driver's test when he entered a Ferrari at Indianapolis, but he eventually took it with other rookies and passed it.)

Alan headed a group which circulated a petition, signed by 60 persons, designed to blackball Miles. The petition, along with wires and phone calls, was directed to National HQ in Westport, Conn. Johnny von Neumann started a counter petition to aid Miles' cause.

THE ANTIS WIN

The anti-Miles movement paid off. Miles was informed by Jim Lowe, National secretary, that his application had been refused, returning his check without explanation.

Ignacio Lozano, local SCCA prexy, said the board of directors had approved Miles' application (firsted by von Neumann and seconded by Johnny Porter) and sent it to National, yet this same Lozano signs a letter, which follows, stating Miles has been nixed.

The letter says it was the unanimous opinion of the board that Miles' conduct was not up to snuff, yet Porter, a member of the board, seconded the motion that Miles be accepted.

This writer contacted some 10 leading local SCCA members. All denied having seen it. "Obviously I wouldn't sign it, since I approved his application," Lozano stated, yet he inked the letter giving the Britisher the harpoon.

ALAN REFUSES

Alan did say he had a copy of the petition, but refused to reveal its contents. In so many words he indicated it was not MOTORACING's business.

This writer wired James H. Kimberly, National president, in Chicago, and George C. Rand, secretary of the Contest Board, in Fairfield, Conn.

Rand wired back that Miles was unacceptable, that contents of the petition were considered
(Continued on Page 9, Col. 3)

Oakes, Beverly Hills, Calif.; Jim Gilletrist; Venice, Calif.; Johnny Tolan, Denver, Colo.; Howard Kelley, Inglewood, Calif.; Ski Redican, San Bernardino, Calif.; Johnny Baldwin, Oakland, Calif.; Walt Faulkner, Long Beach, Calif.; Norm Hall, Hollywood; and, Don Horvath, Riverside, Calif.

Jimmy Bryan, Phoenix's favorite speed son, has been given a special release from his contract with Car Owner Al Dean, whose machine Bryan will gun in the Indianapolis 500-miler. Bryan will engage in a 3-lap match race with another well-known driver —possibly Bettenhausen or Parsons, Mohamed indicated.

Ken Miles Ouster

(Continued from Page 4)

club business and not available for release.

Kimberly didn't even have the courtesy to answer, which was no surprise at all to this writer, who got an insight into his modus operandi last time he was here at March Field. But he's a millionaire.

SCCA DAMAGED?

They claim that as CSCC prexy Miles was instrumental in damaging the SCCA. We know a lot of other CSCC diehards who haven't exactly blown kisses to the SCCA.

The 60 names on the petition constitute about 14 per cent of the local SCCA membership. And this was what allegedly guided National in rejecting Miles!

This writer personally doesn't care if Miles races for the CSCC, SCCA or WPA, but he feels the SCCA booted the whole she-bang but good . . . proving that the outfit is at least consistent.

Following are the local letter to Miles and his answer:

SPORTS CAR CLUB OF AMERICA
Los Angeles Region, Inc.
March 7, 1956

Mr. K. H. Miles
2810 Sunday Trail
Hollywood 28, California
Dear Sir:

Please be advised that at a meeting held on March 1 the Board of Directors of the Sports Car Club of America, Los Angeles Region, Inc., upon recommendation of the Regional Contest Board, agreed to suspend you from participation in events conducted by this Region for a period of six calendar months, commencing Feb. 26, 1956.

It was the unanimous opinion of both the Board of Directors and the Regional Contest Board that your conduct prior to and during the recent Palm Springs Road Races was not in keeping with the standards of courtesy, sportsmanship and observance of authority upon which this Club was founded and was based on the following occurrences:

1. At Safety Inspection held at Continental Motors on Thursday, February 23, you carelessly or deliberately caused a person who was attempting to speak to you to be thrown to the ground, very nearly causing serious injury to him, when you drove into the inspection pit at an excessive rate of speed.

2. Your departure from the Safety Inspection area was dangerous and discourteous and reflected unfavorably upon the Sport.

3. On Saturday, February 25, you left the fuel pit in a careless and unsafe manner.

4. On Sunday, February 26, you profanely refused to obey an order of a member of the Regional Contest Board that you report to the impound area at the conclusion of Race 8.

We wish to state that your letter of apology was read to both boards and was duly considered. In the interim since the decision of both boards was reached we have received a copy of a letter addressed to you advising you that your application for membership in this organization was not accepted. Consequently, we have tabled action at this time.

Very truly yours,
SPORTS CAR CLUB
OF AMERICA
Los Angeles Region, Inc.
(Signed) IGNACIO E. LOZANO
President and Regional Executive

March 9, 1956
Sports Car Club of America
Los Angeles Region, Inc.
Los Angeles 15, California
Dear Sirs:

I acknowledge receipt of your letter of March 7, 1956.

The regional executive, Mr. Lozano, informs me that since I am not a member of your organization I am denied the elementary right to defend myself against the false and damaging accusations contained in your letter.

Since I learn that your letter has been circulated to various parties whose good opinion I value, I am forced to advise you that I do not acknowledge the truth of your statements.

Dealing with your various charges in detail:

1. I deny that at safety inspection I deliberately caused a person to be thrown to the ground. The party in question is well known to me and informs me that he clearly stated to your representatives that I was entirely blameless in this matter as I obviously had no knowledge that he was leaning on my stationary car when I was called into the inspection bay by your officials. I deny and can bring witnesses to support my denial that I drove into the inspection bay at an excessive speed.

2. I deny, and can bring witnesses, including the owner of the property, that my departure from the safety inspection area was in any way dangerous or discourteous.

3. I deny, and can bring witnesses, including the General Petroleum representatives, that I left the fuel pit in a careless and unsafe manner.

4. I deny that I refused to obey an order given by a member of the Regional Contest Board to report to the impound area. I did point out to him that we were in the middle of changing wheels and plugs in readiness for the next race, and told him that we would report to the impound area as soon as we were finished. On reporting to the impound area, I was in-
(Continued on Page 10, Col. 3)

(Continued from Page 9)

formed by your officials that there was no point in my reporting to the area since very few people had bothered to report.

My letter of apology was a personal apology to the above mentioned representative of your Regional Contest Board for words which passed between us, and I object to the implication in your letter that the apology covered the various false charges that you have made, which charges I do not admit and defy you to prove.

I contend that your letter is malicious in intent and indicative that the satisfaction of personal dislike is more important to your board members than the welfare of the sport which you are reputed to uphold.

Sincerely yours,
(Signed) K. H. MILES.

By the mid fifties, the Santa Barbara venue was attracting some serious competitors. Here, Ken in the Von Neumann Porsche Spyder is passing Dr. William Eschrich in his Lotus Mk IX with a 1500cc Porsche engine. On Saturday, September 1, Miles won the semi-main followed by Richie Ginther in another Von Neumann Spyder, Jean Pierre Kunstle in a Spyder and Dr. Eschrich. On Sunday, September 2, Miles won again with Kunstle second and John McLaughlin in an Osca MT-4 third, then Ginther and Eschrich. *Photo from the Sports Car Journal archive.*

*MG CLASS F SPEED RECORDS
August 18, 1956

DISTANCE	INTERNATIONAL STANDING	NATIONAL STANDING	NATIONAL FLYING
25 K	*	142.38	155.04
25 M	*	146.90	155.02
50 K	148.39	148.39	155.05
50 M	150.89	150.89	155.13
75 K	*	150.39	155.11
75 M	*	152.39	155.24
100 K	151.75	151.75	155.24
100 M	153.12	153.12	155.34
200 K	153.66	153.66	155.43
200M	154.30	154.30	*
250 K	*	153.99	155.38
250 M	*	154.22	*
300 K	*	*	155.39
300 M	*	142.96	143.46
400 K	*	*	*
400 M	*	143.12	143.51
500 K	142.97	142.97	143.45
500 M	141.17	141.17	141.47
1000 K	141.66	141.66	141.91
1000 M	141.46	141.46	141.61
2000 K	141.86	141.86	141.97

INTERNATIONAL			AMERICAN STANDING		
Time	Distance	MPH	Time	Distance	MPH
1 hr.	153.98	153.98	1 hr.	153.98	153.98
3 hr.	429.2614	143.09	3 hr.	429.2614	143.09
6 hr.	853.6681	142.28	6 hr.	853.6681	142.28
12 hr.	1700.5653	141.71	12 hr.	1700.5653	141.71

AMERICAN FLYING		
Time	Distance	MPH
1 hr.	155.38	155.38
3 hr.	425.9703	141.99
6 hr.	855.5774	142.60
12 hr.	1700.5653	141.81

Photos from the Peter Miles collecton

During August 1956, Captain George Eyston (right) and Ken Miles (left) took an experimental MG to the Bonneville Salt Flats. Dubbed the MG No. EX-179, the car was in Class F, for unsupercharged engines of 1.1 to 1.5 liters. There were two engines, one, the "sprint" for an all-out speed run and the other, the "duration," was less modified for an endurance record. Using the "sprint" engine, Captain Eyston attained an average speed of 153.69 mph for a ten-mile run. Ken Miles and Eyston, taking three-hour turns, ran for six hours at 121.63 mph and for twelve hours at 120.87 mph. These were new American records. A new international record was set for twelve hours from a standing start with an average speed of 120.74 mph. *Photo from the Ron Ellico collection*

Ken Miles driving Lance Reventlow's 1100cc Bobtail Cooper during practice at Pomona in June 1956. *Photo by Ken Parker from the Warren Olson collection*

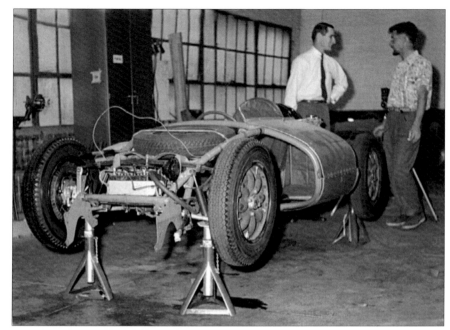

The Von Neumann Bobtail Cooper in the shop undergoing the installation of the Porsche engine. *Photos from the Sports Car Journal archives*

At the first running of the Pomona races held in June 1956, Lance Reventlow showed up with a new Bobtail Cooper with an 1100cc Coventry Climax engine. Even though at the time, Lance was young and inexperienced, he showed what the car could do. In Race 6 for modified cars under 1300cc on Saturday, June 23, Reventlow was third overall. In Sunday's main event for modified cars under 1500cc, he was 8th. In those days, competition in these categories was stiff.

Having joined the Von Neumann team, Miles drove a Porsche Spyder. But lo and behold, there were other drivers in Spyders also with outstanding talent. Sunday's event was won by Richie Ginther with Ken one second behind.

Impressed with the performance of the Reventlow Cooper, Ken asked Lance if he could give the car a try during practice. Ken always wanted to race a car that could win, preferably every time. Even though he had great success in R-1, when he saw the writing on the wall, he built R-2. Similarly, when it became apparent that the old MG engine couldn't compete with the wonderful 4-cam Porsche mill, Ken went with Von Neumann, the Porsche distributor.

Ken making some last-minute adjustments on the Bobtail Cooper.

The installation of the Vasek Polak tuned 1500cc 4-cam Porsche engine in the Cooper turned the car into a world beater. Ken, always personally involved in the mechanics of cars he drove, was meticulous in his approach to race preparation. Right out of the box the car won and it won big.

Its second outing was the November 1956 Paramount Ranch event. Ken and the Cooper not only won the under-1500cc main event, but also the over-1500cc modified main. Both times, Miles beat out Jean Pierre Kunstle, a former SCCA National Champion, in a Porsche Spyder. J.P. was arguably as good a driver as Miles at the time.

Starter Cy Yedor (right) congratulates Ken for his main event win.

Ken's win of under-1500cc as well as the over-1500cc main events at the November 1956 Paramount Ranch races attracted a lot of attention. Paramount, close to urban Los Angeles, was a popular venue and there were a lot of spectators.

At the 1956 Nassau Speed Week, Miles was 4th in the big race. The first of 1957 was held at Pomona on January 19-20. On Saturday, Miles won in what *Road & Track* called "the amazing Cooper-Porsche," with Bob Drake in a Cooper Climax second. The best Porsche Spyder was J. P. Kunstle in third. On Sunday, the results were the same. In the main event for over-1500cc cars, Miles and the Cooper were running with the front group—that included Phil Hill in a Monza Ferrari and Carroll Shelby in a 4.9—when he lost it on Turn 4, crashed through the snow fencing and injured a spectator.

Local as well as the international press covered both events. Monthly racing magazines trumpeted the Porsche-beating Coopers. The problem was that Ken was driving for John von Neumann and the Cooper belonged to John. The Porsche engine that powered the Cooper was one of the rare and valuable 4-camers.

John Von Neumann, sole owner of Competition Motors, was the Western States distributor for Porsche and Volkswagen. The success of the Porsche automobiles was (and is) important for sales of production cars. To put it mildly, the Porsche factory in Germany was not pleased with the publicity that came from the Miles wins. The factory demanded that Von Neumann stop racing the Cooper-Porsche. He complied and sold the car to Stan Sugarman. The January 1957 Pomona was the last time Ken ever drove it.

The first Cooper-Porsche was that of Pete Lovely of Tacoma. It was called the "Pooper." Others were called Cooper-Porsches.

Famed photographer Lester Nehamkin shoots Ken and the Cooper.

On November 17-18, 1956 at Paramount Ranch, Ken Miles scored a triple in the Cooper. On Saturday, he won the under-1500cc semi-main, on Sunday he again won the semi-main and then went on to win the over-1500cc main event. *Photo by Allen Kuhn*

Ken had a decidedly playful side that manifested itself from time to time. In the photograph above, by Jim Sitz, he horses around at the Fall 1956 Santa Barbara with Rolf Wuetherich, a mechanic who worked at Competition Motors. The photo at the right, from the Dick Van Laanan collection, was taken during a California Sports Car Club Christmas party. The man on the left with the checkered shirt is Arnie Cane (the club starter), next to him is Dick Van Laanen, the cute girl is Joanie Yedor (Cy Yedor's wife), to Ken's right is Richie Ginther.

Miles was back in the Von Neumann Porsche Spyder at the March 9-10, 1957 event at Paramount Ranch. On Saturday it rained. At the start of the under-1500cc main event, Bob Drake in Joe Lubin's Cooper-Porsche led Ken by a few seconds for the entire race. Drake repeated on Sunday, five seconds ahead of Miles. The question in everyone's mind was, would Ken have won in the Cooper-Porsche? *Photo by Allen Kuhn*

During Ken Miles' days of driving Porsche Spyders for John Von Neumann, Bob Drake was one of his closer competitors. Here, Ken leads Bob at the May 4-5, 1957 race at Hourglass near San Diego. This was the first race held at what was then part of Miramar Naval Air Base. The course itself was designed by Miles with assistance from Dick Van Laanen. The event was conducted by the San Diego Region of the SCCA, which had just been granted regional status by the national office. The weekend was limited to cars under two liters. On Saturday, Miles led Drake, driving Joe Lubin's Cooper Climax, by five seconds. On Sunday during the main event, Drake retired with a slipping clutch and Ken lapped every other car in the field. *Photo by Bob Norton*

At the June 15-16 Paramount Ranch, Ken pulled another clean sweep, winning not only the under-1500cc semi-main, but also the main event itself. During the main event, however, he broke a rule and was disqualified by the race judges. The chief judge was Al Moss. See his remembrance of the incident on page 27. Also read the editorials on the next two pages. *Photo by Allen Kuhn*

Ken Miles was occasionally involved in controversies. There were those who hated him, prominent among them was Gus Vignole, editor and publisher of a bi-weelky newspaper, *Moto-Racing*. In order to provide a flavor of those times, two editorials are reprinted here. The first is from *MotoRacing*, the second from the *Sports Car Journal*.

With regard to the incident wherein Ken was disqualified at Paramount Ranch, see the remembrances of Al Moss on page 27. Al was the person most directly involved.

Vol. 2–No. 18   (Published Bi-weekly)   44   15c   June 28-July 5, 1957

EDITORIAL

L'Affaire Miles

THERE IS an old line something to the effect that if you give a guy enough rope, he will hang himself.

Kenneth Miles, the Britisher who to all intents and purposes is paid to drive by the Porsche distributor here

One of the most thought-provoking letters ever received by MOTORACING, written by Charles Beaumont, appears on Page 2. It deals with the vitally-important subject of safety and the view taken by Ken Miles. Don't miss it!

and competes under the guise of "amateurism," has just about reached the end of his rope.

Miles is president of the California Sports Car Club – elected by that group's Board of Pharaohs and not by the general membership.

Miles and other members of the claque are now in the midst of strenuous efforts to "muscle in" on Northern

(Continued on Page 2, Cols. 4-5)

(Continued from Page 1)
California road racing by staging a race at Laguna Seco, near Fort Ord and Pebble Beach, Nov. 9-10. Work on that course is not due to begin until August.

This has most of the SCCA boys up north in arms.

Miles and some of the other Cal Club brass have been buttering up a fellow by the name of Lou Gold. They had him in fine tow, thank you, the other day at the Paramount races. Gold is associated with the Del Monte Properties in Pebble Beach and, although by his own admission, knows little or nothing about road racing ("Honestly, I didn't even know the CSCC existed until a couple of weeks ago!"), we want Mr. Gold, in particular, and the readership, in general, to know the latest about Miles.

At Paramount, Miles—the president of the club staging the races, mind you—was DISQUALIFIED for infraction of the rules after he had won the under-1500cc race for modified cars.

He was **KICKED OUT** of the race by his **OWN CLUB.**

Elsewhere in this issue you will find the reason and other particulars.

Nothing in Entry Blank on This

Also at Paramount, Miles tried to engineer a deal whereby the first three finishers in the under-1500 race would be permitted to race in the over-1500cc feature.

Now, mind you, this was in direct contradiction to the conditions and rules as printed in the entry blank and in the program.

In case you are not hep, let us bring you up to date. Paramount is a narrow, tight two-mile course. The finely-tuned Porsche which Miles drove was a natural shoo-in in the under-1500. Unlike Fangio, Miles never drives just fast enough to win. He goes all-out to win by as many LAPS as he can.

Give the public a show? That is a laugh!

He belted the field handily in the under-1500, but before he did he started to exert his muscle as president of the club to make for the allowance in the big-bore.

Drivers of the bigger cars, naturally aware that Miles had a fine chance to also win their race on that **PARTICULAR TYPE OF COURSE**, resented it.

There was a furious stink about it. A petition was even drawn up. Drivers threatened to pull out of the main event, and justifiably so. The petition was presented to Lew Kaplan, co-chairman of the race.

Miles threatened to place the Porsche on the trailer and get out. He said he wanted to race and he wanted to WIN. Otherwise, I'll pick up my marbles and go home!

The pits were fuming, not only from the insufferable heat but from Miles' latest caper.

At any rate, the race officials strangely acceded to the tion (signed by several big-bore drivers) and staged the **AS IT WAS SCHEDULED AND NOT AS MILES WANTED IT**

So here you have Miles rebuked by his **OWN CLUB** Issue. And after he won the under-1500, you have Miles pres

IFIED BY HIS OWN CLUB.

On top of this, last year the L.A. Region of the SCCA threw Miles out at Palm Springs. And earlier this year, he was thrown out by the San Francisco Region at Stockton. And a few weeks ago he was thrown out by the Salt Lake Region.

Recent Ouster National SCCA Edict

The important thing is that his most recent ouster at Salt Lake came on orders from the National Pharaohs at Westport.

The significance of this is obvious. It means, from all indications, that Miles is through for the time being as a driver in practically every race in the United States except those staged by the California Sports Car Club.

This is one of the reasons why Miles is fighting tooth and nail to have the Cal Club stage more races—even if they are out of the club's territory and are an out-and-out infringement on the rights of others.

The water level is getting up to Miles' neck.

But they are getting wise to him—even a segment of the Cal Club. The petition at Paramount is a perfect example.

It appears that the day is not too far distant when the water level will be up to his Brittanic brow—and he will be through with road racing as it is now conducted in this country.

There has been much talk among members to **THROW HIM**

(Continued on Page 5, Cols. 2-3)

(Continued from Page 2)
OUT as president of the Cal Club. There has been talk that he will resign. So far he has not.

Nor are these recent capers anything new.

During his first reign as **PRESIDENT** of the CSCC—yes, fantastically enough, he has been named to the top spot **TWICE**—he was protested at Palm Springs for illegal fenders and use of questionable fuel in one of two gas tanks on his mount. He changed the fenders—the equivalent of admitting an infraction of the rules —and was absolved of the other charge.

At a Palm Springs Victory Banquet he created a scene when he pushed his trophy back and told Dr. Karl Brigandi, "You need this more than I do."

At one tech inspection he bombed his car out of the joint, almost running over a driver. There are witnesses to this.

At Torrey Pines another terrific howl went up when he charged through the pits at a fantastic speed.

When his name is mentioned at two firms that formerly employed him, there is a furor.

Let The Northerners In On It

The editor of an English motoring publication rousted him for some charges he made in a letter to that sheet.

He personally told this writer he "had something to do" with Gold Suit's stock car races being scheduled on the same day as the SCCA races at Palm Springs last November.

Then, last January, came the reprehensible jacket-throwing episode at the Pomona races.

Copies of this issue of MOTORACING are being sent to every member of the San Francisco Region of the Sports Car Club of America.

And a special copy to Mr. Lou Gold, whom Miles and the club have approached regarding the staging of the Fort Ord races.

If Miles is successful with the northern venture, fine. Maybe he can stay up north, although it is indeed a terrible thing to wish him on those fine people in the Bay Area.

The only good thing about pain is the relief from it.

The only good thing we can say about Miles, although at the moment the hope is slim, is that we might be relieved of him.—GUS V. VIGNOLLE.

EDITORIAL

NEARLY all of the past issues of MOTORACING, a local racing publication, have been devoted, almost exclusively, to criticising the California Sports Car Club or a member of its board of governors. The last attempt, dated June 28 - July 5, takes the cake. Our policy, up to now, has been to completely ignore this publication. This we can no longer do. Almost every issue, like certain EXPOSE rags, has blasted either the club or one of its directors—based largely on half-truths and inuendos. The latest in question is the president of C.S.C.C., Ken Miles.

Miles makes front page news in this latest discharge. Across the top of the front page, in large bold type, reads: "Illegal Pit Stop Disqualifies Miles; Daigh Races to Victory". Not more than a few inches away is a front page editorial (in red) attacking Miles violently. The editorial, in effect, says nothing.—But to the uninitiated casts reflections on Miles as an individual. In one part it becomes so disgustingly thick that it asks the reader: "If you don't believe us, ask his former employers". What kind of Yellow journalism is this?

KEN MILES IS, WITHOUT A DOUBT, ONE OF THE MOST CONTROVERSIAL INDIVIDUALS IN MOTOR RACING TODAY. HE HAS BEEN INVOLVED IN SEVERAL DISPUTES. HE IS OUTSPOKEN AND SOMETIMES VERY OPINIONATED. HE IS LIKED BY MANY AND, UNDOUBTEDLY, DISLIKED BY OTHERS.

Ken Miles made an illegal pit stop at the recent Paramount Ranch Road races. This writer, personally, made a survey of over 15 competitors at Paramount on Sunday. The concensus of opinion among the drivers was that Miles should have been disqualified. The officials, before the race, carefully made it clear to all drivers that there was to be no pit stops on the straightaway, violators would be disqualified. Miles, practically one full lap ahead of the nearest competitor, slowed down, near the start-finish line, and was handed a glass of water. **He did not stop.** This was considered, by many, as a "pit stop" and subsequently was ruled on by the board of governors as an illegal procedure. MILES WAS DISQUALIFIED. Big deal. Miles was disqualified by his own club. Do we mean to say that Miles does not have enough control over his own club to dictate to them what to do and say? Miles was also delivered a "slap on the hand" by the board of governors of the same club (of which he is president) that same day. Ken wanted to race his under 1500 c.c. car in the big-bore event. He was told that he could not run, both by members of the contest board and members of the board of governors. WHAT DOES THIS PROVE — IF ANYTHING, IT PROVES THE IMPARTIALITY OF THE C.S.C.C. BOARD OF GOVERNORS.

Certainly Ken Miles is controversial. He likes to have his own way. But who doesn't? I don't always agree with Miles — but on the same hand I don't always disagree with Miles.

continued on page 10

EDITORIAL—continued

KEN MILES IS THE BEST UNDER 1500 c.c. PILOT IN THE UNITED STATES. HE IS A VERY PROMINENT MEMBER OF THE BOARD OF GOVERNORS OF THE CALIFORNIA SPORTS CAR CLUB — THEY ELECTED HIM PRESIDENT (HIS THIRD TERM). HE IS ONE OF THE LEADING EXPONENTS OF IMPROVING SAFETY FOR THE RACING DRIVER. HE WORKS HARD AS PRESIDENT OF C.S.C.C. AND WAS VERY INFLUENTIAL IN HELPING THE CAL CLUB BUILD THE ONLY TWO PERMANENT RACE COURSES IN EXISTENCE ON THE WEST COAST. HE IS PRESENTLY NEGOTIATING SEVERAL ADDITIONAL COURSES FOR THE C.S.C.C. HE IS SINCERE IN HIS EFFORTS AND HAS CONTRIBUTED GREATLY TOWARD MAKING THE CAL CLUB AS GREAT AS IT IS.

Early this year the board of governors of the Cal Club were given an overwhelming vote of confidence by its 1500 members. All of the board were returned with the exception of Lew Kaplan, who was probably one of the least controversial of the whole board — DESPITE A BITTER AND CONTINUAL ATTACK ON THE BOARD BY **MOTORACING.**

Ken Miles has not been accepted as a member of the Sports Car Club of America and is, therefore, banned from racing in any S.C.C.A. sanctioned event. Reasons for this ban are still very unclear in this writer's mind. No reason for the refusal of Mile's application to S.C.C.A. is given, either by the local region S.C.C.A. or the National. The real reason, of course, is not obscure. Ken has been working very hard for, and in the interest of, the California Sports Car Club—and well he should. It is a known fact that had Miles participated in the recent S.C.C.A. Salt Lake races licenses OF ALL OTHER COMPETITORS WOULD HAVE BEEN REVOKED.

MOTORACING stated, in another article, that Ken Miles offered an out and out loan of $25,000 to SCRAMP, an organization composed of Monterey Peninsula businessmen and chambers of commerce interested in building up that region, for the development of a race course at Laguna Seca, on Government property near Fort Ord. THIS IS COMPLETELY FALSE. Miles, on behalf of C.S.C.C., has offered to UNDER-WRITE up to $10,000 of the proposed $100,000 loan being made to SCRAMP by local Monterey Banks. Another $10,000 is being underwritten by personal friends of Ken Miles. Several influential northern individuals have also offered to underwrite part of the $100,000 loan. This is not an unreasonable offer by Miles. C.S.C.C. is responsible for nearly this much money every time they sponsor a race. Pomona, alone, requires close to $18,000 investment each time a race is held there.

I deplore the use of isolated incidents for casting shadows on people's character. Dragging out dead horses, using them over and over again is unnecessary and unethical. Because certain staff members of MOTORACING personally do not like C.S.C.C., or some of its directors, is no reason they should use the publication to inseminate these bitter resentments. For those of you uninitiated in the background, it may be of interest to know that the firm of Vignolle & Powell, who between them comprise MOTORACING, both in management and ownership, previously handled public relations for the C.S.C.C. Their vitriolic attacks commenced with the issue of MOTORACING following termination of their services. WHAT SIGNIFICANCE DO YOU ATTACH TO THIS? Miles has acted rashly at times, but each time I hear about one of those isolated incidents they become more and more exaggerated. This, again, is unnecessary.

* * *

While on the subject, we would like to mention that in the issue of MOTORACING, mentioned above, there was a letter to the editor (which exceeded MOTORACING'S limit of 100 words by close to 1000) taking issue with Ken's recent series, for this magazine (Journal) on safety. IT IS TRULY UNFORTUNATE THAT CHARLES BEAUMONT, THE AUTHOR, DID NOT SEND US A COPY OF THE LETTER. FOR WE WOULD BE MORE THAN HAPPY TO PRINT IT. CONTROVERSY IS A GOOD THING. THE FACT THAT MR. BEAUMONT DISAGREE'S WITH MILES IS THE PRIVILEGE ALL AMERICANS ENJOY.

* * *

Here in the West, one of the hottest subjects of the "Bench-racing societies" is the new Riverside International Motor Race Way, which, you might recall, received a considerable amount of publicity last year. The idea was conceived by restauranteur Rudy Cleye, put on paper, then presented, in various ways, to potential backers. Originally the project was designed as a multi-million dollar venture to construct one of the largest raceways in the world and would include drag strips, oval tracks and a genuine Grand Prix racing course over five miles in length. The idea was good, the intentions sincere, but after an enthusiastic beginning the whole idea seemed to drop into obscurity. Until recently nothing more was said about the course until rumor had it the course was again "under construction."

Apparently, the necessary financial backing was obtained and the course began construction. We had the opportunity to view the course, first hand, recently with the result that we were pleasantly amazed. Much of the pavement is laid and the course is approximately 65% complete. Although it gets extremely complicated when we discuss who is exactly behind the venture it is fairly certain that Rudy is definitely an important part of the organization and that wealthy John Edgar, well known race car owner, is in for a healthy part. Several others claim they are connected in one way or another. It is hoped that the whole thing will not become bogged-down by "too many chiefs," for the track is an important mile-stone toward getting a full fledged Grand Prix race on the West Coast and should play a very important part in racing activity for all major racing organizations. (Complete story and pictures on the new track will appear in next month's Journal).

DICK SHERWIN

Dick Sherwin in 1997.

The controversies involving Ken Miles were deeply disturbing to me personally. For I sat in the middle!

My own position was awkward since I served a term as a director of the SCCA Los Angeles Region. It's leaders, Lindley Bothwell and Jim Peterson, were my close friends.

In addition, Dick Sherwin and I were best friends. He and I started the *Sports Car Journal* as an extra-credit college project.

Through it all, however, a cross word never passed between Ken and me. I don't even remember a disagreement.

Even though Ken Miles dropped out of high school at age 16, he was very literate. Always an inveterate reader on all sorts of subjects, Ken was an excellent writer. The only problem was that he couldn't type and his handwriting was atrocious.

Unfortunately this characteristic was demonstrated directly to the author of this book. During the second half of the fifties, Dick Sherwin and I published a road-racing magazine, the *Sports Car Journal*. For a time, Ken wrote essays in a column titled, "racing review." Due to the passage of time, many of them seem dated. The following, which appeared in the March 1958 edition, however, may still, perhaps, apply. (Reprinted with the permission of Dick Sherwin.)

racing review By Ken Miles

". . . Don't laugh! There will be some drivers reading this in a hot flush of indignation!"

If ever you want to see a baffled expression creep over a man's face, catch a Sports Car Driver and ask him why he goes racing!

There is, after all, a whole variety of excuses that a man can come up with for playing golf; there are certain social advantages to membership of a good club, most club houses have an excellent and well patronized bar, and the member can always plead that the exercise that he gets from hitting the little ball and then going in search of it is good for his health, though just where the golf buggy fits into this scheme of things I have never been able to discover. Furthermore, since his wife doesn't enjoy the game, he spends the afternoon in congenial company of his own choosing.

The enthusiastic swimmer can claim not only the advantages of strenuous exercise but also the opportunity to contemplate the female form in a more or less untrammeled state, though the growing skill and ingenuity of Rosemarie Reid and others tends to sow the seed of suspicion in a field where heretofore the truth stood forth or fell unsupported. The Chess player or Contract Bridge enthusiast can point to the development of his mental powers, the Hunter to his contribution to the Nations food supply (or Surplus), the Fencer to his skill in warfare (of a slightly archaic nature), and even the professional racing driver gets paid for the risks he takes, but what can the amateur Sports Car Driver say? The present generation of sports cars, unlike those of yesteryear, require no great physical effort to drive for the duration of our short races, and though reasonably good health is a prerequisite of good driving, the driving cannot be said to contribute to it in any

way, whilst any advantages that might accrue in the way of reduced alcohol consumption, cutting down on the cigarettes to improve one's reaction time and so forth are more than cancelled out by the damage to the nervous system and increased blood pressure brought about by interviews with the race officials, trying to keep up with the latest changes in the regulations and worrying about how you are going to explain to your wife that you really must have a new set of Pirellis even if they are 155 dollars apiece.

Drivers' wives seem equally confused as to their reason for encouraging, or at least tolerating the expenditure of time on the car and money on the products of Pirelli rather than Schaparelli. The most widespread reason seems to be, "It's better to have him chasing other cars than other women, and at least I get to go to the races." Reading that authoritative masterpiece from the pen of a one-time competitor "Hero Driver," one might be forgiven for assuming that a fast lap around the course was merely the prelude, the aperitif as it were, to a fast lap around the bedroom, the attraction lying under the bedcover rather than under the bonnet, but this viewpoint fails entirely to explain the complacent attitude of the wives or the midnight hours spent reconstituting shattered machinery so it can run the next day.

Since it is no good asking the driver why he races, the only way of finding out is to study the species from the protection of some suitable disguise, probably the easiest being to pretend to be one of them to study behavior.

In view of the fact, regrettable but inescapable, that most of them enter races knowing full well that they haven't the slightest chance of winning, the urge to victory can be the motivating factor in only a very small minority of cases; all sorts of hidden motives must be at work to persuade a man that it is worth the expenditure of such prodigious quantities of time, money and enthusiasm in order to consistently finish last or last but one. Ostensibly we are all racing just for fun, but it is curious to see how some of the enthusiastic amateurs regard their "fun."

There is, admittedly, a certain atmosphere of glamour surrounding racing, an air tinctured with the color of high powered cars with exotic foreign names like Ferrari and Mercedes-Benz, and their sometimes even more colorful owners, and some people bask in the reflected glory of association with these names; they dress the part, talk the language, hang around the faster cars and their owners and enjoy making believe that they are part of the production; they don't drive themselves but know far more about racing than the drivers do and impress their friends with their knowledge of why you didn't win the race and what they would have done had they been driving your car. Many people consider the races chiefly as an excuse for a weekend vacation, a social event, and an opportunity to down unprecedented quantities of liquor, a prime chance to shoot the bull with others of their kind. Sometimes they find that unless they race themselves, they are left at the post in the bar stool racing so they enter one or two races a year chiefly in order to maintain their status as an expert, their right to speak with authority when the merits of various cars and drivers are under discussion. Then we have the hairy chested He-man, the type who uses racing to prove how brave he is, how courageously he conducts himself in this "dangerous" sport; careful observations will reveal that he substitutes recklessness for skill and foolhardiness for good judgment, he constitutes a hazard to every other driver on the track and is the first to go on his head when the unexpected happens; he objects to the presence of women in the "men's" races on the grounds that his natural and instinctive chivalry would prevent him from pushing them around (he calls it "driving hard") like he does the other men.

The publicity hungry are easy to spot, at least to the experienced eye, though to really appreciate them you have to be an official of the race. If they own a 1500cc Porsche then it is obviously unfair to allow a 1600cc Porsche to run in the same race; if they own a Mercedes-Benz then they complain about the unfair advantage of engine size enjoyed by the Corvettes; they own a little car . . . and don't want to run with the big cars because they feel that their sterling performance would be overshadowed by the big cars; they own a big car . . . and don't want the smaller cars to run in the same race in case they should be beaten by a smaller car. When they have a runaway win they complain that the announcer spent all his time talking about the battle for second place . . . they didn't win, and they complain that all the announcer was watching was the battle for the lead. Don't laugh! There will be some drivers reading this in a hot flush of indignation!

Amongst the more sympathetic types is the "Concours racer." He genuinely loves automobiles and considers the sports-racing car as the epitome of everything that a sports car should be. Owning such a car is his lifelong ambition, and should he be fortunate enough to own one, he dedicates his spare time to maintaining it in better than new condition, and, incidentally, chiefly to provide himself with an excuse for owning it, he also enters it in races.

Most difficult of all to identify, since he owes allegiance to no particular class of car, may be the consistent winner or never win a race, own a worn out MG or a spanking new Maserati, is the man who is racing just because he likes it, races because he enjoys the satisfying feeling of driving a car better than the next man, enjoys the feeling of competition, the satisfaction of carrying through a difficult and dangerous maneuver in safety, enjoys exercising his judgment, his eye for a line, his feel for the changing surface of the track, his quick reaction to potential hazards and his ability to drive quickly, but safely. He is interested more in doing the very best he can within the limitations of his machine than in collecting a trophy for "the best driver with a red car" and more interested in improving his driving technique than putting on a demonstration of recklessness and daring. Rarely spectacular enough to catch the eye of the Press, yet always in the forefront of competition, rarely in trouble yet always driving to the limit of his ability, he is the unrecognized backbone of our sport, and from his ranks are recruited the future great names of racing. He is the "little guy" in the sense that he rarely makes the headlines, and yet he turns up at the races with a properly prepared car and a desire to drive as well as he can, learn as much as he can and some day drive a winning car.

In those days, usually there were two main events for modified cars. After the fifties, what were then called modified cars are now referred to as sports-racing cars. Almost always, each of the two main events were one hour in duration. They followed one another, the first for cars under 1500cc displacement, the second for cars over 1500cc. Front-running finishers from the smaller displacement event were usually invited to run in the main event for the cars over 1500cc.

It was a foregone conclusion that Ken would compete in both main events. This meant driving for an hour, taking a short breather and then going for another hour. This never fazed Miles, as he was a fitness fanatic.

During 1956 and 1957, Ken won one over-1500cc main event and came in third overall three times. Keep in mind that the competition usually included Phil Hill, Richie Ginther, Carroll Shelby, Bob Drake and the like in the latest from Italy.

MILES, VON NEUMANN PART COMPANY

Ken Miles, foremost under-1500cc sports car pilot, and John von Neumann of Competition Motors last week parted company.

Miles was practically unbeatable behind the wheel of von Neumann's Porsche Spyders since joining Competition Motors early in January, 1956, as "field representative."

Asked if Miles would continue to drive the marque, von Neumann said he had made no commitments for the Porsches. "We just go from race to race," he said.

Miles raced for von Neumann last week at Pomona, losing on Saturday to Jean Pierre Kunstle, but winning handily on Sunday.

Von Neumann said there was nothing to rumors Chuck Daigh would drive for him in the upcoming three National SCCA races. He is not entering the Porsche. (Editor's Note—This was before Daigh was banned for racing in a pro event.)

The association between Ken Miles and John Von Neumann lasted two years: 1956 and 1957. During that time, Miles hung up an amazing record, cementing his title as the premier U.S. under-1500cc sports car pilot.

During the Von Neumann tenure, Ken scored 41 podium finishes. He was first 24 times, second 12 times and third 5 times.

The November 1, 1957 edition of *MotoRacing* reported that Miles and Von Neumann had come to a parting of the ways.

The story goes that Ken resigned in anger. The first event for the just-opened Riverside International Raceway was held on September 21-22. Ken had his heart set on winning, but Von Neumann was in Europe at the time and had left instructions that none of his cars were to compete in his absence. So Ken had to sit it out.

The first event for the new association was the Santa Barbara Memorial Day under-1500cc modified main event. Miles finished both days in second place with Jack McAfee winning in Stan Sugarman's Porsche Spyder. The Sugarman car had a later RSK engine while the Zipper had an RS. This situation continued throughout the year.

Ken continued driving for Otto Zipper until his employment with Carroll Shelby. When Ken got a car with an RSK engine, things improved. From 1958 through 1963, Miles won 38 of the 44 races he entered. *The photo below was taken by Allen Kuhn.*

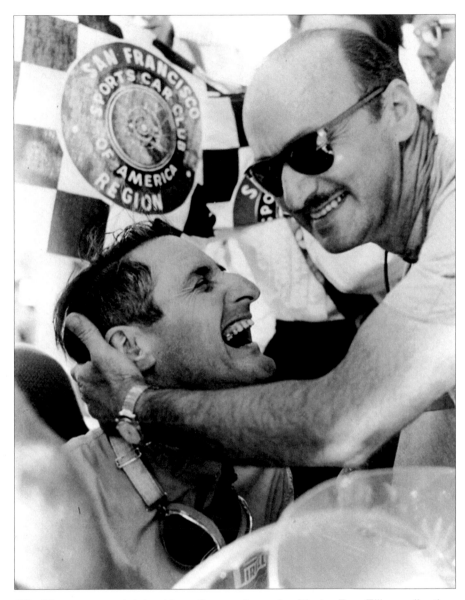

Otto Zipper congratulates Ken after another win. *Photo: Ron Ellico collection*

After a relationship that had its ups and downs, John Von Neumann and Ken Miles parted company at the end of 1957. Early the following year, Ken secured a ride with Bob Estes-Otto Zipper organization, which included a Porsche dealership in Beverly Hills.

CAROL ZIPPER REMEMBERS

Ken Miles wasn't exactly a hidden book or a shy person. One did not have to guess his intents or thoughts. I don't mean to imply that he was transparent, far from it. He was usually quite straightforward; but there was frequently a subtlety that implied a bit more meaning than was always apparent.

Ken was never dull. He was frequently great fun, witty in his own way, sometimes exasperatingly stubborn and always, always, "Ken." One did not have to hear that familiar voice or see the peculiar shape of his head, but if a third person were telling a story about someone without naming names, you always knew if it was about Ken. I guess what I'm trying to say is that he was distinctive in many ways. Maybe he was not distinguished, but rather, always identifiable.

I don't think Otto knew Ken before my husband acquired the RS Spyder from John von Neumann. All I do know is that it was almost like a package deal. Otto bought the car for our dealership, Precision Motor Cars, and Ken came along for the ride.

I know very little about racing sports cars. Heck, my introduction to anything that went round and round on a track was seeing Bob Estes' (Otto's partner) 35B Bugatti up close and personal. I learned to drive the "racing way" (Very, very poorly; the straight-cut gears on the car were a terror to me.) in Otto's 37A Bugatti . . . on Sunset Boulevard . . . wearing thong sandals. It was great fun. Needless to say, I never, ever entered a race.

The point is, though, that I never realized the intensity that enters into the world of driving fast in competition. Ken's intensity was probably unrivaled. His desire to win seemed to be an unquenched thirst. Just before a race, I remember staying well away from him.

I'm not certain, but I speculate that winning in his own "home built" specials probably gave him more satisfaction than any other conquests. It's really a shame, due to the Ford hierarchy, he didn't have an unadulterated win at Le Mans.

Ken and Otto delighted in each other in many ways, not the least of which was figuring ways to extract an advantage over the competition whether it was to slightly alter a gear ratio or changing tire pressures. They delighted also, I swear, just by the sheer arrogance of their confidence in each other. And believe me, they were both arrogant, not only about their ability to set up a car but also Ken's great talent in driving the "bloody thing." Otto greatly minded losing Ken,

the first time to Carroll Shelby (Although Otto didn't begrudge Ken the chance to go on to "bigger and better" things.) and then, of course, to that horrible accident.

I didn't actually see all of Ken's races in the Spyders, but I do remember cooking breakfast in our moving motor home while driving from Monterey to Laguna Seca. Otto was driving and Ken was yelling at him to, "Hurry, hurry, we're late." All the while, I was trying to perk coffee without getting scalded. They both jumped out and ran on foot while we were still outside the paddock, leaving me to get the whole shebang through the gates without the proper credentials.

I remember going to Mexico City for the races at Avandaro. I imagine that Papa Rodriguez stage-managed that. Montezuma's revenge hit me while Ken and I were sightseeing. Ken wasn't affected; I think he had a cast-iron stomach. The next morning, Otto, Patrick deGoldsmith and Ken all paraded past my bed saying how sorry they were to be leaving me alone. Ken's parting line was, "Well, we did come all the way down here to race. You wouldn't want us to miss that just because your tummy is upset, now would you?" I replied, "Of course not, Ken. That's what you all come alive for and I know it."

I still don't really understand, and never will, what it is about motor vehicles going fast around impossible curvatures of a road; the smells of grease, raw gasoline, burnt fuel and smoking rubber that so entrances so many seemingly intelligent people. I do know, even with all the disappointments and cost to family life (My children still complain that I missed things with them because I tagged along to so many races.) it was damned good fun.

Years later, I remember helping polish old cam shafts by hand, sighting the rich and famous who flocked around exotics and all the oohs and aahs over our 540K Mercedes or a one-off Ferrari. Still, it was the roar and the race that really thrilled us. Ken Miles so vibrantly brought it all to life, not just for himself, but for all of us.

Note: Otto Zipper died on February 3, 1979. Carol is his widow, now living in Santa Ynez, California. Bob Estes died in 2002.

Photograph on the next page by Allen Kuhn

On August 31, 1958, Miles drove Jack Brumby's 121LM 4.4 Ferrari to fourth overall in the main event at Santa Barbara. Bill Krause in his D-Type Jaguar (#127) failed to finish. According to Jim Crow in his article in *CSCC Notes*: "The field for the main event at the 10th Santa Barbara was the finest display of sports car racing machinery ever seen in the west. With three Testa Rossa Ferraris, one 4.4, a DBR-2 Aston, a D-Jag, the new 3-liter Offy Scarab, a pair of DB3S Astons, a Lister Corvette and a handful of powerful American Specials including the Balchowsky Buick, the Murphy Kurtis Buick and Chuck Porter's Mercedes Corvette, it couldn't miss being one of the great races of the year." Max Balchowsky ended up scoring his first main event win followed by Richie Ginther in John Von Neumann's Ferrari 250TR and then Von Neumann himself in a 500 TRC Ferrari. *Photo by Allen Kuhn*

Ferrari enthusiasts will be happy to learn that Ken Miles, did, in fact, race Ferraris on occasion. While early on he was known primarily as a small-car driver, he drove a Parravano's 4.9 at Santa Barbara on September 3-4, 1955. On Saturday, he came in third behind Ernie McAfee and Phil Hill, both in Monzas. On Sunday the car failed to finish, but Ken managed to win the semi-main in his "Shingle."

At the Seattle Seafair that year, he scored another third in Allen Guiberson's 375, this time behind Carroll Shelby and Hill. At the fall 1958 Santa Barbara, Ken managed a fourth in Jack Brumby's 4.4 121LM.

Skip forward to 1962. In a production Ferrari SWB, Miles achieved a string of first-place victories at Riverside, Pomona, Reno and Laguna Seca. He also chauffeured Otto Zipper's 500TRC to first overall at the spring Santa Barbara. The only other outing in the car was at Reno where it was a DNF.

Ken in Otto Zipper's Ferraris. Above: the 250 GT SWB production car, Below: the 500 TRC. *Photos: from the Ron Ellico collection*

Six-hour races had been a short-lived tradition at the old Torrey Pines venue near San Diego. On Saturday, November 22, 1958, the California Sports Car Club revived the idea of staging endurance races at the Los Angeles County Fair Grounds near Pomona. During the fifties and sixties, sports car races were held in the parking lot which today is the site of NHRA drag races.

Carlyle Blackwell was a prominent Hollywood still photographer who indulged himself by acquiring and racing expensive sports car. Although he enjoyed himself immensely, Carlyle was far from a front runner in spite of the quality of his machinery. On this occasion, Ken Miles was persuaded to co-drive.

With a lack of publicity, few name drivers and heavy iron entered. After the gaggle sorted itself out, Don Hulette in his Corvette Special (which had started life as Bill Pickford's Jaguar Special), pulled more than a minute ahead of Blackwell, who had taken the first turn at the wheel. When the cars pulled in for gas, Eric Hauser took over for Hulette and Ken started driving the D-Type. And that's all she wrote. Miles stretched his lead to over five laps.

On Sunday, Miles scored a clean sweep in the Estes-Zipper Porsche RS. Because the field for the main event was not very large,

Race Chairman David Bracken asked Ken to compete in the main event for over-1500cc cars rather than the one for the smaller cars.

Miles won, even though Richie Ginther was driving Jack Nethercutt's 2-liter Ferrari plus Jack Graham in a DB3S Aston Martin.

This weekend demonstrated Ken Miles' ability to drive and win in larger displacement cars. Previously, he was thought to be only a small-car specialist. Those nay-sayers had forgotten that Ken had driven the Troutman-Barnes Special in 1954 with some success. Of course, in the following decade, Miles demonstrated world-class expertise in Cobras and Fords. The weekend also highlighted his ability to jump from one car to another without missing a beat.

The photo at the left shows the start of the 6-hour race. The Carlyle Blackwell D-Type Jaguar driven by Blackwell and Ken Miles is on the far right. Next in line is a Corvette Special with Don Hulette and Eric Hauser, a Wadsworth Coventry Climax with Tony Settember and Keith Hoyt, Bob Bondurant and Fred Grant in a Corvette and John Dixon and Joe De Muniz in a Maserati. *Photo: John Dixon collection* Below: Miles in the Blackwell D-Type. *Photo: Sports Car Journal archives*

Not to be outdone by the *Los Angeles Times*, its rival newspaper, the *Los Angeles Herald Examiner* decided to sponsor a professional sports car race in Southern California. Held on March 8, 1959, the event was sanctioned by the FIA and the USAC. A host of heavy iron and quick pilots entered such as Jerry Unser in Mickey Thompson's Kurtis-Pontiac, Dan Gurney in Frank Arciero's 4.9 Ferrari, Carroll Shelby in John Edgar's 5.7 Maserati, Max Balchowsky in Ole Yeller (#70), Chuck Daigh in Bill Murphy's Kurtis, George Amick in Chuck Porter's Chevy-powered Mercedes Special and Jim Jeffords in his Scarab. Others included Jim Rathman, Lloyd Ruby, Tony Bettenhausen, Roy Salvadori, Maurice Trintignant and Count von Trips. Nevertheless, lap after lap, various favorites dropped out and at the end, Ken Miles (#50) crossed the finish line 35 seconds ahead of Sam Weiss in another Porsche Spyder (#55). *Photo from the Peter Miles collection*

With prize money of $10,000 (a lot in those days), the July 19, 1959 Kiwanis Grand Prix at Riverside attracted some top sports car entrants as well as a few professionals like Lloyd Ruby, Billy Cantrell, Duane Carter and Johnny Mantz. It was so hot that Cantrell and Bill Krause (4.5 Maserati) retired from heat exhaustion. Richie Ginther in Eleanor Von Neumann's 4.1 Ferrari of California (she got the Ferrari agency in the divorce settlement) (#211) won followed by Sam Weiss in a Porsche RSK and Miles in the Zipper RSK. A lot of heavy iron and quick pilots failed to finish. *Photo by Allen Kuhn*

Ken Miles in the Zipper RSK Porsche won the main event at Santa Barbara on September 6, 1959. Behind Ken is Don Hulette in his Chevy (formerly Jag) Special (#204). Dick Morgensen is in the Ferrari Testa Rossa (#46). Next to him is Frank Livingstone in the Eliminator (#184) . Behind Livingstone is Ak Miller in his Devin Olds (#311). Morgensen finished 17 seconds behind Miles and Livingstone was third more than a lap back. (Yours truly is back in the pack.) *Photo by Allen Kuhn*

Very occasionally, Ken would drive a Formula Junior. His first experience with the new formula was in Jean Pierre Kunstle's Stangulini at the Memorial Day 1960 Santa Barbara event. He finished third in a race limited to the class.

Previously, Miles had had little experience with open-wheel cars. At the October 1954 Palm Springs, he raced a Formula 3 Cooper and scored third in the formula car event. According to the program, the car was entered in Ken's name, but since he only raced it this one time, he was most probably not the owner, whose name seems to be lost in the mists of time.

On June 15, 1958, Ken drove a Talbot-Lago Grand Prix car owned by Bob Estes and Otto Zipper at a hill climb held at Lake Arrowhead in the mountains above San Bernardino in Southern California. He scored third fastest time of the day.

At the end of 1960, Miles started campaigning a Dolphin Formula Jr. owned and entered by the Dolphin Engineering Co. The photograph above and on the opposing page show him in the works car. His first outing was at the November 1960 Pomona and he won the formula race, probably much to the delight of the Dolphin people, who were trying to market their cars.

He raced a FJ Dolphin a number of times the following year. Unfortunately, the Pomona finish was his best. In the 1961 Mexico City, he failed to finish; at the March Pomona he was second, but at Stockton in April he again failed to finish. Miles raced for Dolphin two more times with even less impressive results.

Miles was involved in an attempt to construct Formula 3 cars before he came to the U.S. If he ever raced one is not known.

Photos by Bill Norcross

Back at Pomona again on July 9, 1961, the best Ken could manage was fifth. This was his last race in the Formula Junior. *Photo by Phil Binks*

Chuck Porter built a special combining a Mercedes Benz 300SL convertible body and chassis with a Chevrolet V8 engine. The car was fast, but not always reliable. On May 29, 1960, Ken Miles drove Porter's car at Santa Barbara. He dropped out with engine trouble while in second. *Photo by George Robitschek*

During 1961, Ken drove a Porsche RS61 occasionally for Frank Zillner of Wisconsin in U.S. Road Racing Championship events. This photograph by Bob Tronolone was taken at the Los Angeles Times-Mirror Grand Prix for Sports Cars at Riverside on October 15. The competition was world-class. World Champion Jack Brabham won the race followed by future World Champion Bruce McLaren with Jim Hall third. Miles finished seventh overall and second in class. Oliver Gendebien was first in class with such fast feet as Jack McAfee, Dan Gurney, Jerry Grant, Stirling Moss and George Follmer behind them.

With their Formula Junior on the market, Dolphin Engineering ventured into the realm of sports car construction. Fitted with a 1500cc Porsche engine, Miles drove it on a few occasions. Unfortunately the results were not even as good as those he achieved in the Dolphin Formula Junior. *Photo by Allen Kuhn*

Ken Miles made one foray into the ranks of stock car racing, albeit on a road course. On November 3, 1963, at Riverside, he was running in sixth place when co-driver Fred Lorenzen took over and finished in eleventh. *Photo from the Peter Miles collection*

Somehow or another, the California Sports Car Club persuaded the Los Angles city fathers and Walter O'Malley to let them stage races in the Dodger Stadium parking lot. Three were held, all in 1963 and Ken won two of the main events in Otto Zipper's Porsche. Next to Miles is Bob Challman in a Lotus 23 (#2). Future Formula 1 driver Ron Bucknum is in an MGB (#31); Frank Monise is in his Lotus 23 (#244); Jay Hills is in another Porsche (#288). *Photo by Allen Kuhn*

In 1961 and 1962, Ken drove part-time for Sunbeam distributor Rootes Motors. He was often entered by a local dealer such as Larry Reed Sports Cars, one of the oldest foreign car dealerships in the area. Larry's first store was in Westchester; later he expanded to a second location in Torrance.

Reed started by racing sports cars himself. His first race was Southern California's first road race after WWII, the 1950 Palm Springs. In 1954, Larry retired from competition and started sponsoring cars for others to drive. While Ken was his most successful entrant, he was not the most famous. World Champion Jack Brabham drove for Reed in the October 1962 Los Angeles Times Grand Prix in another Alpine.

Due to his experience with Sunbeam Alpines, perhaps the seed was planted for the Sunbeam Tiger. As is demonstrated in the photo to the right, even with Ken Miles at the wheel, the Alpine just didn't have enough power to consistently win races. In this picture by Bill Norcross, Charlie Gates leads Miles at the Spring 1962 Riverside event. On both Saturday and Sunday, the best Ken could do against the Porsches was third in the F-G-H production race.

Larry Reed is standing to Ken Miles' right. The person to Ken's left appears to be Cy Yedor. *Photo by Bill Norcross*

Rootes Motors made the most of Ken's driving Sunbeams. This ad appeared on the back cover of the program for the Los Angeles Times Grand Prix held on October 13-15, 1961.

Both of these photographs were taken by Allen Kuhn at Santa Barbara. The one above shows Ken catching Davy Jordan in his Porsche Speedster; the one below shows Ken after making the pass.

CHARLIE AGAPIOU REMEMBERS

I first met Ken Miles early in 1962. I had apprenticed as a truck mechanic in the U.K. My brother and I came to the U.S. After spending about a month in Florida where I couldn't find a job as a truck mechanic, we came to Los Angeles, looking for work. I was walking down a street in North Hollywood and saw a sign, "English Mechanics Needed." So I went in and said I'm looking for work. Ken needed someone pretty badly, so I started the next day. I had no idea who Ken Miles was or that he had anything to do with racing. My brother, Kerry, ended up there too. Jean Stucki was already there.
This ad was in the June 1962 Riverside program.

Ken was a fabulous boss. His shop did basic mechanical work, mostly on foreign cars. Miles always had a few of his own projects going. When I arrived it was the Sunbeam Alpine that Ken was racing

for Rootes. That's how I got involved in racing. Part of the job was to go to the races and pit for Ken. Of course, since the races were usually only a half hour long, there wasn't much work to do, but it was a lot of fun.

Charlie Agapiou sitting in a customer car in front of Jim Parkinson's Italiano Motors and Ken Miles Ltd. with a pizza kitchen in between. *Photo from the Charles Agapiou collection*

We went to the races in Ken's 1950 Ford station wagon. He always drove it flat out, never slowing down, even when pulling the trailer. It would scare the daylights out of me. Ken won almost every race. We watched him drive and helped him. Basically, we were not race mechanics. The number of things I learned from Ken was unbelievable. It was an education. Ken was always teaching. Even when he drove for Otto Zipper, he took me with him. Any question I asked, he would always answer with great patience. He wanted people to learn.

At the beginning of 1963, Ken drove a few races for Shelby whilst he still had his own shop. I think Carroll was sort of testing Ken to see how he would do in a Cobra. Obviously, he proved himself right out of the box. When Ken would come back to the shop from racing a Cobra, you could tell he was absolutely delighted.

After moving the shop three times, the IRS showed up and put big locks on the doors. So I was out of a job. One day Ken called and asked me to come work with him at Shelby American. I said, "I'm not a race mechanic." He answered, "Don't worry, you can bluff it." It turned out to be like a dream come true. It was incredible, the highlight of my life. I was almost always part of the team that went to the races too.

The year I remember most was 1966. Ken won Daytona and Sebring. Then came Le Mans. It was the most important event in Ken's career. The strategy that Carroll plotted was for Dan Gurney and Ken to be the rabbits. It was their job to get the Ferraris to break. Dan went into the lead from the start. Ken couldn't get his door closed because it was jammed. So he made a pit stop during the first lap and we fixed it, but now he was dead last. So Ken decided he would catch up. As I remember, he broke the lap record several times. So finally, he caught up with Dan and they were running together. But a water line broke on the Gurney car and he had to retire, thus putting Ken in the lead.

McLaren was several laps back and then Ronnie (Bucknum). At that point, Miles was running away with the race and he started to pace himself. Ken was four laps ahead when Bruce came in for a pit stop for a brake rotor change. We had spare rotors bedded in for each car to prevent vibration. But there weren't any bedded rotors for the McLaren car. So I used the bedded rotors intended for Ken's car. Then Ken came in for a rotor change and all I had to install were new rotors. After a lap, he came in again and told me that there was tremendous vibration from one of the rotors. He made another lap whilst I located another new rotor and when he came in again, I took off the offending rotor and put on another new one. This solved the problem, but Ken had lost a couple of laps, but he was still ahead.

Then they decided they would dead heat the race. This was fine with Ken. When the race ended, I thought it had ended in a dead heat and I was trying to get the car into the winner's circle. When the officials wouldn't let me into the circle, I found out that McLaren had been declared the winner because at the start, he had been lined up farther back and had, therefore, traveled the most distance.

When I was in Europe, I saw all of the great drivers of the time: Andretti, McLaren, Hill. As a GT driver, I think Ken was better than all of them. Since he never drove in Formula One, we'll never know how he would stack up. But especially in the GT40 MkIIs, he was so good, when we went to a race, we knew he was going to win. At Sebring in 1966, he drove the open roadster. Gurney was in the coupe. For most of the race, Dan was ahead of Ken. When Ken came in for a pit stop, he told me, "Dan has a heavier car, he's going to have problems." I said, "What do you mean, Dan's car is running perfectly." It was amazing. On the last lap, Gurney's engine puked. I was stunned. How could Ken have known that would happen?

Miles was a complete gentleman. He had a great sense of humor. Even in the early days when there were all sorts of problems, even then, nothing seemed to faze him, even the IRS.

When Ken went to work for Shelby as competition manager, he wasn't supposed to drive. His job was to test, get the cars ready and manage at the races. But he was completely frustrated in the pit. He just couldn't stand there and watch. He had to be in one of the cars. Finally, Shelby let him drive.

I absolutely loved Ken; he taught me so much. He was like a father; he was my teacher, my mentor. He meant everything to me. After he died, I went on working for Shelby for a few months, but it wasn't the same. I got a job somewhere else. Ken Miles was fabulous, a great man, a wonderful engineer. He died on my birthday, August 17. I miss him; even today I miss him.

Opposite page: Charlie Agapiou standing with Ken in a Maserati Birdcage at Laguna Seca in October 1962. Entered by the Maserati distributor, Ken raced the car only two times. *Photo by Lester Nehamkin*

THE SUNBEAM TIGER

An article by Bill Carroll appeared in the July 1978 edition of *Road & Track*. Editor Tom Bryant had asked Bill, who was the PR person for Rootes at the time, to write about the origins of the Tiger to accompany an article Tom wrote titled, "Sunbeam Alpine & Tiger." Bill was also an assistant editor of the *Sports Car Journal*.

The Tiger, A marvelous automotive fantasy comes true
BY WILLIAM CARROLL

"Gads, what a great car if it only had power," was the plaint of Jack Brabham and Stirling Moss, pleading for more power in Sunbeam Alpines they raced. Rootes Group management, listening well, took a quick look at Humber, Singer, Hillman, Comer and Snipe iron, then decided they'd go elsewhere. Which was Modena, Italy, and the lair of the prancing horse.

Meetings were underway with Ferrari in late 1962. The object: a Ferrari-designed cylinder head with Weber Carburetion that would make Alpines hum. As you can imagine, Rootes sales executives were riding high with plans for marketing Alpines "Powered by Ferrari." But for naught. One day the Italian word was, "We have nothing further to discuss." Rootes staffers sadly returned to their island and left the Ferrari dream behind.

Failure of Rootes' power search was soon made known to their U.S. west coast manager, Ian Garrad. As Carroll Shelby explains in his book *The Cobra Story* (Trident Press): "The idea of dropping a Ford engine into a Sunbeam Alpine originated in the minds of Bill Carroll and Ian Garrad who was the west coast representative for Rootes."

With encouragement, Ian moved to boost Alpine sales against Corvette, Austin-Healey and Jaguar. His first step involved a "precision" instrument of questionable antecedents.

The instrument, a genuine wooden yardstick, was Ian's measuring tool as he eyeballed the engine room of an Alpine. There seemed room for more cylinders so one of his staff began "engineering research" in nearby Buick, Chevrolet and Ford

showrooms. There, hood up, head under and curious salesmen dancing about, the Rootes man busied himself yardsticking Detroit engines and recording his dimensional findings. The last stop, at a Ford dealership, was Rootes' bottom line: A 260 V-8 appeared to be just right. Ian's next worry was how to stuff a Ford into Rootes' future.

So far it had been easy but accomplishing the dream was something else. Fortunately, Lord Rootes' son Brian, the Group's talented export manager, was in California for a convention. Ian hustled to San Francisco and broke the news of his V-8 project. Sales-wise Brian leapt at the package for its obvious positive support of Rootes' marketing plans. "Okay . . . I'll get the money, somehow, from our advertising account . . . but don't let my dad know what you're doing."

Back in Southern California the next day, a handshake agreement between Shelby and Garrad priced the job at a maximum of $10,000 for engineering and construction of the first car. Delivery? Within eight weeks!

Never one to waste time, Ian had an engineless white 1963 Alpine delivered to Shelby's Cobra plant the following morning. But Ian couldn't wait to learn how good an Alpine could be, so another car was scheduled.

This time Ian called fellow Britisher, Ken Miles, who had a neat shop in Hollywood. Sure, he'd be glad to do a swap for $600. "Bring over a car," Ken said. A green Alpine was soon at Ken's where a Ford 260 V-8 with automatic transmission was shoveled onto fabricated transmission and engine mounts. The V-8's fan was left off for lack of room and two electric Jaguar fans were bracketed in front of the radiator. The driveline was cut to fit and, as Ian recalls, with plumbing and electrics, that was it.

This first-ever Alpine V-8 was completed over one weekend by Ken and Ian. Sunday, near midnight and raining cats and dogs, found Ken hauling on the Hollywood Freeway like there was no tomorrow. Ian tells me that when they returned, the usually taciturn Ken said, "This will really sell." What did Ian think? "I was looking for a place to change my underwear," he says.

The rest of the article goes on to tell about the Shelby conversion as well as the rest of the Tiger story. Ken Miles had no further involvement.

WILD

Let a wild beast like this Sunbeam Tiger go flat out, there is no pussy footing around when you're at the wheel of a Sunbeam Tiger, thanks to it's powerful Ford V-8 engine, with sustained cruising speeds of 115 miles per hour. A driving position and controls perfected by track action. Ford V-8 engine with automatic twin-choke carburetor . . . Ford 10 inch diameter clutch . . . 4 speed all synchromesh transmission . . . large capacity drive shaft, modified suspension, rack and pinion steering, sports type front seats, plus vacuum servo-assisted braking. All these outstanding features are included in the wildest tiger roaming, The New Sunbeam Tiger. Powered by Ford.

FROM THE RACING FAMILY OF SUNBEAM BY **ROOTES MOTORS.**

SUNBEAM
ST TIGER
POWERED BY FORD

Following is an article that appeared in the October 1963 edition of *Road & Track* and is reprinted here with permission of Editor Tom Bryant. A great deal of the information is duplicatory, but I decided to include it because of the numerous quotations from Ken.

KEN MILES - OUTSPOKEN, OUTGOING & USUALLY OUT IN FRONT

By W. Lee Tomerlin

Thirty-three years ago, British-born Ken Miles first tried a competition machine. Ken was just 11 years old. "A friend of mine in England owned and raced a 350-cc trials motorbike," he relates, "and even at such tender years, I was aching to get aboard." After much coaxing, Ken's friend finally acceded, which set the stage for the first Miles High-Speed Adventure.

"It didn't last long," he says, his sharp, nearly hawk-like countenance breaking into a crooked grin. "And when it was over, the bike had an interesting, but totally non-functional shape: something like a pretzel. I'd had a dispute over right-of-way with a lamp post—the first of several similar arguments I was to lose with inanimate objects as time went on."

For the next few years, young Kenneth H. J. Miles had little opportunity to pursue his newfound hobby, though he rarely missed attending events held reasonably near his home. He never lost his enthusiasm, however, and today he is one of the West Coast's most familiar figures as he strolls, teapot often in hand, through the working pits.

Ken's penchant for tea (most Britons prefer coffee, American humorists notwithstanding) stems from long-established habit: his father and grandfather, both lifetime residents of Sutton Coldfield, England, are owners of the Henry Miles tea-importing-exporting-blending firm located there. Even today, Ken's father, Eric Miles, sends him cans of select tea.

Ken's leanings, however, were never toward the family business. In fact, from the day he first mounted his friend's motorcycle to the present, his professional bent has been solely toward mechanics. This interest, plus an incompatibility with formal schoolwork, conspired to force his life onto an entirely different road. In following this inclination, he quit school when he was 16 years old to take on a 5-year apprenticeship with Wolseley Motors.

He began to make his way up through the firm, first doing janitor work, then fabricating, then assembling—and always learning. But he was never to finish that indenture, begun in 1935. The impact of World War II jarred him loose from the company, and by August of 1939 he was a tank mechanic in an armored regiment of the Territorial Army. Turing the conflict he saw duty in Scotland, Holland, Belgium, was on the Normandy beach on D-Day plus three, and was a member of the invading Allied forces which finally penetrated Germany.

"I also operated an anti-aircraft gun, foraged for fresh eggs behind enemy lines, and passed out millions of 'liberated' Reich marks—not dreaming that after the war they'd still be good."

While still in the Army, Ken returned to his hobby of speed and organized the first of a series of motorcycle and sailboat races in the Baltic Coast region.

"I stayed in the Army until 1946," he says, "then tried to return to Wolseley Motors. I was bumped because of the 'Officer Replacement Program' (Miles was discharged a sergeant) but by then it didn't matter; I was determined to make mechanics my life's work. A philosophy I'd developed in the Army intrigued me: A machine is inflexible by nature, and can't change its method of defense. And when it acts stubborn—which is nearly always—all a man has to do is change his method of attack; which, being flexible, he is able to do."

When Ken was forced to leave Wolseley for the second time, he took up tool machining to provide bread and butter for himself and Mollie, whom he had married during a furlough in 1942. He also bought his first "sporting" car, an ancient Frazer-Nash, into which he installed a Ford V-8 engine. He describes his competitive efforts (primarily hill climbs) in the car as "mildly successful, at least for a beginner," and was seen in events at Prescott, Silverstone, Brands Hatch, and others. But the machining and the Frazer-Nash both came to their ends early in 1948: the car expired during a race ("Another argument, this time with the side of a hill," Ken says) and Morris offered him a job as development engineer.

He stayed there a year, then took a more lucrative position with Webley & Scott, armaments manufacturers, in research and development. The job was a good one, Ken admits, but it seemed to be taking him ever further from the type of work he most desired to do, so when John Rawley came up with an idea for building half a dozen 500cc specials, Miles jumped at it.

"We worked on the machines for six months, 14 hours a day, seven days a week, until they were done," Ken remembers. "The effort we expended cannot be estimated, but it all seemed well worth it when we were finished. The cars were beautiful! We had paid extremely close attention to detail. For instance, we nickel-plated the high-stress tube frame and suspension members. The result was beauty, all right—and ruin." The plating process had served to cause embrittlement of the steel, and the first time the cars were raced, each dropped out with a broken frame.

The venture was disastrous to Ken's finances, already somewhat strained by the birth of his and Mollie's son, Peter. "Things were headed for a pretty pass," he remembers, "when I heard about an MG distributor in California who was in trouble. Seems his service manager didn't know a great deal about the car's insides. They offered to let me take over, and within days (just before Christmas, 1951) I was on my way."

After about six months in this country, during which time he was busily engaged in organizing his shop and settling his family in its new home, he was able to take a stock MG to Torrey Pines, where he placed fifth in class. "Not bloody good," he said, so he took the MG out again, this time to Stockton. And when he returned home the second time he was bearing a class trophy. "Better" he decided and entered a MkII in two Carrell Speedway races. Each time he departed with yet another first-in-class trophy. "Great fun," he enthused, "now let us go faster."

So Miles began work on the first of his famous specials, this one powered by a modified MkII engine coupled to a TD gearbox: the original "No. 50." His success with the car was quick and complete. Finished just before a Pebble Beach event in 1953, Ken placed first overall in the under-1500cc modified race, the first of a long series of such victories which were to thoroughly establish him as the West Coast's finest small-car driver. Phoenix, Golden Gate Park, Stockton, Chino, Moffett Field, Santa Barbara, Madera, Long Beach, March Field, Palm Springs, all saw him win that year; but the (Palm Springs) Spa victory marked the end of the triumphal march for the little special. Ken sold it immediately afterward—having in mind plans for an even faster machine: the "Flying Shingle."

During most of 1954 Miles drove a modified TF, while at the same time heading the California Sports Car Club for his first year—to the general delight of its driving members, and the general dismay of its established officials.

"I had the idea that most of the Cal Cub officers were not very much interested in sports car racing," Ken says, "and, in fact, were mostly interested in bossing other people around. I set out to correct this—and I'm afraid a few people felt I was stepping on their toes."

Ken's speech is full of British phraseology and during his tenure of office, it was also full of sharp criticism. As Mollie puts it candidly: "Ken is not a diplomat. He's honest—often brutally so—and will speak out, no matter who is in the way. If he doesn't like you, you know it!" To wit: "I have a great deal of respect and admiration for Jack McAfee . . . on the race track!" Or: "A club, like CSCC, which doesn't organize races has very little right to call itself a racing club, has it?"

But apparently the rest of the membership felt he was doing the job well. He was re-elected again for 1955, the year his second MG special was ready for the starting line.

"That's when my 'injured parties' got their own back," Ken relates. "We took the 'Shingle' out for its first big race, at Palm Springs. The debut went well; we won. However, after the race I was disqualified by those same officials, because the rear tires were exposed a fraction of an inch too much."

"It was a case of malice; sheer, unadulterated malice over a technical point so small as to be negligible. But the car's performance was excellent, and we felt that the 4500 man-hours, which had gone into its construction, had not been wasted. We were ready to take on all comers!"

Miles did just that, driving the car—a reworked MG employing a modified TF engine and TC gearbox, and identifiable by its extremely low profile—to victory against far larger displacement competition. Soon news of his prowess reached executive ears in Britain—aficionados had started calling him "Mr. MG"—and he was signed to co-drive the then-new MGA prototype at Le Mans. Miles and John Lockett brought the car in 12th overall, ahead of some more powerful and ostensibly faster marques among the 69-car starting field. (They crossed the finish line eight laps ahead of the fastest Triumph!)

Later that year Ken sold his Shingle, at the same time leaving MG. "A new general manager and I had a meeting of minds," Ken muses. "He decided he wanted to run my service department, and I decided to let him." Ken went to work for John Von Neumann, Hollywood racing enthusiast and Porsche-VW dealer. It was von Neumann who put Miles into his first Porsche Spyder.

"My inaugural ride in the Porsche was a bit more exciting than I had bargained for, I'm afraid," Ken says. "On my very first practice session I got somewhat carried away with the car's potential, and went into a corner too fast. Seeing a stack of hay bales, I made for them . . . only to discover they were on the other side of a ditch. A rather cruel joke, I remember thinking at the time; and then I hit the ditch, flipped right over the hay bales and hit a cement wall! The car was an utter ruin, but I was able to stand up by myself—so Johnny gave me another 550 Spyder."

Ken verified Von Neumann's confidence by finishing third overall in the main event the next day; but this was just the beginning. Soon Miles was collecting first-place trophies at Bakersfield, San Diego, Santa Barbara and Paramount Ranch. In addition to the Spyder, he also drove his third special that year, a Porsche-powered Cooper. The car was extremely fast, so fast that on one occasion (at Paramount) Ken drove it to an overall win in the over-1500cc main event!

"But the Porsche people had become very indignant over the 'Pooper,'" Ken chuckles, "because it was faster than their RS550s. They brought some pressure to bear, so we sold it to McAfee, but it never seemed to run properly for him . . ."

Ken was back in Porsches for the 1957 season, during which he won eight main events, a class second at Sebring, and the under-1500cc West Coast Championship. He was also elected to head CSCC for his third and final term. "Quite likely the reason they returned me to office was because during my two previous years as president the club had run no less than 20 races," says Ken.

In 1958 Von Neumann retired from racing, so Miles started driving Spyders for Otto Zipper. His initial efforts were not very successful: McAfee, at that time driving a similar RS550, consistently finished ahead of Ken; much to the latter's consternation and bewilderment. The reason finally became known: Jack's engine had been "doctored" somewhat, and was putting out far superior power.

The next two years more than made up for that slack season, however. Ken drove Zipper-owned RSKs and an RS60 during 1959-60, and, as he put it: "I don't remember losing a single race in either of those cars." It was also in 1959 that Ken and his wife became naturalized American citizens.

During 1961 Ken raced an RS61 to two overall victories, another first-in-class, and one class second. The car was then withdrawn from competition by its East Coast owner. At the same time, Ken was driving the early models of the Dolphin F-Jr for a San Diego firm. Ken's assistance as a test driver was instrumental in developing the Dolphin Jr into the highly competitive machine it later became and also led to the latest Miles special, the Dolphin-Porsche owned by Otto Zipper. This car, a Dolphin sports chassis and body with a Porsche engine, has been extremely promising in its early try-outs and those who remember the earlier specials are predicting that Ken will soon be doing the factory-built cars in the eye again.

Also in 1961, in a factory-assisted program, Ken campaigned a Sunbeam Alpine in production car racing, finishing second (surrounded by Porsches) in the pacific Coast Championship's class FP.

During the present season, in addition to running his Hollywood garage, Miles has been one of the team drivers with Carroll Shelby's sensational Cobra-Fords. Enjoying the busy racing schedule of the Cobra team, Miles has campaigned all over the country, a crowd-pleaser wherever he has gone. His successes in the Cobra have been especially satisfying to Ken because he has always enjoyed beating cars he "shouldn't." At Lake Garnett, Ken ran the Cobra in the modified car main event and blew off a good field that included a Chaparral, a new Cooper Monaco, and a lightweight Stingray to win overall.

"These years of racing have taught me many things," Ken reminisces. "One of the most important, at least for me, is that I must never take it easy during a race, no matter how far ahead I may be. If I do, then I'm in trouble, for I've found it impossible to 'turn it on again if my position is challenged. I used to try, and the usual result was that I would either motor off the course, or break my machine. It is maintaining that attitude of constant competition, which has helped me a great deal.

"But I am a mechanic," says Ken. "That has been the direction of my entire vocational life. Driving is a hobby, a relaxation, for me; like golfing is to others. Can you imagine a successful businessman giving up his livelihood for professional golfing? I can't. Also, I am 44 years old—not exactly ancient, but still, for an F-1 driver, 44 is not young." (Ed. note: Ken will be 45 in November.)

Knowledge of Miles' ability to win prizes is not limited to the United States, despite his status as an amateur. He has had several offers of driving contracts from European manufacturers, one of them the Porsche factory in Germany." And someday," he says, "I should like to drive a Formula 1 machine—not for the grand prize, but just to see what it is like. I should think it would be jolly good fun!"

Alert readers will notice the many discrepancies in the foregoing article with other materials in this book. The article is by a respected writer. But it appears that virtually all of the information was derived from an interview with Miles. Inaccuracies, however can seep into aging memories. I know they can into mine. In order to correct the record, the following is offered:

1) "Normandy Beach on D-Day plus three . . " Other sources say D-Day plus one; but what's a day or two? It was rugged.
2) The article implies that Ken's first race in the U.S. was at Torrey Pines. The record shows otherwise; see appendix.
3) The article implies that Ken constructed both MG specials himself. In fact, they were constructed at Gough Industries and owned by Gough. According to Gough General Manager John Beazley, most of the actual work was done by Gough employees Laurenz Melvod and Arne Bjorkli. Ken did the design work. Most of the work was done after hours and all three were paid overtime.
4) "A new general manager (at Gough) and I had a meeting of the minds." Beazley was the general manager and he was not new, having been at Gough prior to Ken's employment. Ken was fired for getting into a dispute with the controller. (But all of us have sugar-coated versions of why we are fired, don't we?) Phil Gough, Sr. gave Ken R-2 in lieu of severance pay.
5) The Porsche-Cooper owned by John Von Neumann was not called the "Pooper." This label was attached to a similar car owned and raced by Pete Lovely. Von Neumann did not sell the car to Jack McAfee, who was a Porsche-VW dealer himself. I hear it was sold to Stan Sugarman in Arizona.
6) A quote implies that Ken did not have a great deal of respect for Jack McAffee off the race track. I have interviewed Jack at length about this and I can also rely on my own memory as an SCCA LA Region board member. Jack, a member of the SCCA Competition Board was an early proponent of roll bars, fireproof suits and full-face helmets. Ken didn't always agree.
7) John Von Neumann didn't retire from racing. Ken quit the Von Neumann team in anger because he was not allowed to compete in the first Riverside event.
8) Yes, Jack McAfee's Porsche engine was "doctored." The "doctor" was the incomparable Porsche magician Vasek Polak. The implication is that there was something illegal which was not the case.
9) The San Diego firm for which Ken drove Formula Junior Dolphins was, in fact, the Dolphin Engineering Co. The Dolphin-Porsche owned by Otto Zipper was not successful. It finished only one race and, some say, led to parting of the ways between Zipper and Miles.
10) Despite Ken's protestations that his ambition was limited to being a mechanic, after being employed at Shelby American, his activities obviously included professional race driver.

THE SHELBY YEARS

This photograph of Ken Miles and Carroll Shelby was taken on March 21, 1964 in the Shelby American paddock during the 24 Hours of Sebring. It illustrates, I think, more than any other picture I have seen, the unique and personal relationship between the two.

At that event, Ken and his co-driver, John Morton, were credited with a 47th overall finish although they didn't finish the race due to mechanical problems. Ken and John were driving the 427 Cobra prototype. This was the first outing for the big-engined car. Even though the 427 didn't do well, the team scored a clean sweep in the GT Class, taking first, second, third and fifth in production Cobras. Davy MacDonald and Bob Holbert were 4th overall and 1st in class in a Daytona Coupe; Lew Spencer and Bob Bondurant were 2nd in a Cobra, with Jo Schlesser and Phil Hill third, also in a Cobra.

It is significant to note that Carroll entrusted Ken with the prototype. Ken's engineering and mechanical skills were equal to his talent behind the wheel. Miles performed most of the testing for Shelby due to his almost mystical sense regarding set up as well as finding anything amiss.

During his active racing career, whenever there was a choice, Carroll always had number 98 on his car. To this day, he considers it his personal number. While other drivers occasionally drove Cobras with 98, most often the number was assigned to Ken.

In the late fifties, AC Cars in England had manufactured a beautiful and competitive sports car. But in 1961, the company lost its source of Bristol engines. Carroll Shelby heard about the problem and sent a letter proposing that AC continue operations, but send cars to California for the installation of an American V8. In 1962, the first car was delivered and Shelby American started operation in Venice, California. In May of that year, the Cobra was introduced to the press.

Cobras were raced a few times in 1962, but without much success. Shelby signed Ken Miles to drive Cobras and he placed 2nd behind Davy MacDonald in another Cobra at Riverside on February 3, 1963. Miles went to work for Carroll full time as competition manager and continued with Shelby until his untimely death.

Before he came to Shelby American, Ken worked on the Sunbeam Tiger. The Sunbeam Alpine originally had a rather lackluster engine. But with a small-block Ford V8, it truly became a tiger. They were not nearly as successful in competition as the Cobras, partly due to the short wheelbase.

Miles went on to drive in more races for Shelby than any of the other team members. His record was also better than any other.

CARROLL SHELBY REMEMBERS

Ken was very unique for me. It seemed like he created a hell of a lot of controversy before he came to work for me at Shelby American. But I always got along with Ken just fine.

After he came to work, he was the heart and the soul of our testing program. He took a pile of shit, the Daytona Coupe (and I hope you print that), and made it work.

The most horrible mistake of my life was listening to Pete Brock on the shape of the Daytona. I had one of the world's most famous aerodynamicist, Denny Howard, and people from Air Neutronics who wanted me to extend the tail. Two years later Porsche showed what should be done with the ass end of a car with the 917. Instead I listened to Peter Brock who wanted to cut the tail off and give a Kamm effect.

The first time it went down the straightaway, Ken said, "My God, the rear end came a foot off the bloody ground going down the back straight at Riverside at 155 m.p.h." It took about three months to get it right. We didn't have money to go to a wind tunnel. We put cotton tufts on it and every one of them went forward. Every day, Ken Miles was out there testing. If he wasn't testing, he was in the shop cutting metal and bending things around. In the end, he made the thing work. Thanks to Ken, John Collins, John Ohlson and Phil Remington, a racehorse was made out of a mule.

Thank God Ferrari was stuck on putting his 3-liter engine in the GTO, so we didn't have a lot of competition. We should have won the World Championship in 1964, but Ferrari caused the last race at Monza to be cancelled. Ferrari, of course, was politically connected in Italy, so when it looked like Ferrari was going to lose the championship, Italy cancelled the race.

The next year, Ferrari ran a 4-liter engine; but it still wasn't a contest. Ken told me Ferrari was going to use a 4-liter early on. Somehow, he got inside information; I never knew where.

Ken was a world-class and the best test driver I ever knew. And I knew most of them in that era. He was also helpful to the other drivers. He reminded me of Fangio in that regard. He would take time to coach the other drivers. All those years before Shelby American, we knew him as kind of a hothead, but it never showed up during the years he was with me.

Since his death, there's not a day in my life that I don't think of Ken Miles. I hope someday we get around to setting up a foundation in Ken's name that helps the things he was so vitally interested in: American Indians and young people trying to break into racing. He understood them and their problems; he helped them.

God rest his soul.

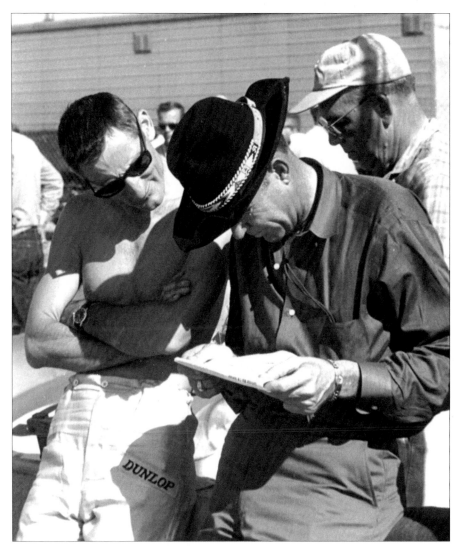

Ken and Carroll at Riverside in 1963. *Photo: Allen Kuhn*

81

The 1963 Shelby American Sebring team. Left to right: Skip Hudson, Ken Miles, Peter Jopp (sitting in car), Lew Spencer, David MacDonald, Carroll Shelby. *Photo: Dave Friedman*

Skip Hudson ended up working for Dan Gurney at All American Racers for a number of years. He died from cancer on June 27, 1998.

Peter Jopp was an English car dealer and driver who made his name in club racing. He had previously driven a Cobra at the 1963 Le Mans.

After Shelby American, Lew Spencer continued to work for Carroll Shelby until 1999 when he retired.

David MacDonald was killed at Indianapolis in 1964. Rookie MacDonald, driving for Mickey Thompson, died in a second-lap multi-car crash and conflagration on Turn 4.

There is little doubt that the success of Shelby's Cobra project was due, not only to Carroll's genius and foresight, but also to the team of outstanding individuals he recruited. Not the least among them was Ken Miles, the lead driver. But Ken was much more than just another driver among a host of talent that included World Champion Phil Hill, Indy winner Parnelli Jones, Dan Gurney, Le Mans winner Ed Hugus, Bill Krause, Augie Pabst, Bob Bondurant, John Morton, as well as such international stars as Jo Schlesser, Chris Amon, Roy Salvadori and Bruce McLaren, to name only a few.

Ken was unmatched as a development driver. He had an uncanny ability to drive a car and then explain to the engineers and mechanics exactly what was wrong or how to make improvements.

Miles had a plethora of engineering and mechanical ability himself. It is significant to note that, although Cobras were raced before Ken arrived, they were not successful until he became involved.

The photograph in the upper right-hand corner shows Miles on the left, Carroll Shelby in the center and Peyton Cramer on the right. Cramer was the general manager of Shelby American. He had been an important automobile industry executive as well as having a large dealership.
Photo: Allen Kuhn

The drawing reproduced here is part of a full-page advertisement that appeared on page 3 of the April 1964 edition of *Sports Car Graphic*. The magazine, no longer in existence, was part of the Petersen Publishing group. The third person from the left with the helmet is Ken Miles.

*We also remove the bumpers, tape the headlights, and paint on the numbers.

COBRA
POWERED BY FORD

FOR MORE INFORMATION WRITE: SHELBY AMERICAN, INC., 1042 PRINCETON DR., VENICE, CALIFORNIA

Bob Holbert (left) and Ken Miles finished first in the GT class and second overall at the Road America 500 on September 8, 1963. *Photo by Dave Friedman*

On loan to the Comstock Team, Ken finished 2nd in the GT class and 7th overall in the Canadian Sports Car Grand Prix at Mosport on September 28, 1963. Canadian Eppie Waitres in another Shelby Cobra finished ahead of Miles to take 1st in GT. *Photo by Don Markle from the Jim Sitz collection*

The first lap of the 1964 12-Hours of Sebring turned out to be a wild melee. The Ken Miles/John Morton 427 Cobra prototype (#1) is in the center of the picture with Ken driving. Other cars are the Barth/Linge Porsche (#41), the Ryan/Beneker Porsche (#39), the Piper/Gammino/Rodriguez Ferrari (#30) and the Hugus/McLanghlin Iso Rivolta Grifo (#5). The Perkins/Eve Ferrari 250 GTO (#82) is just nosing into the frame.

JOHN MORTON REMEMBERS

I was a race fan in my teens, so I knew of Ken Miles even then. When I was 18, I went to Sebring where I saw Ken racing in a Sunbeam Alpine. I remember wondering what a well-known driver like that was doing in such an innocuous old car like that. At that time, I hadn't been involved in the California scene. I knew of Miles from magazines.

When I came to the West Coast, Miles was driving for Otto Zipper as well as the Sunbeam people. Then Carroll Shelby hired Ken and he came to work at Shelby-American. He came on board about the same time as Davy MacDonald. The first race for both of them in Cobras was at Riverside. I recall that Miles was the faster of the two, but for some reason, Shelby wanted MacDonald to win as Davy was slated to be the number one driver. So Ken made a pit stop he didn't need to make so MacDonald could win. After the pit stop, Ken spent the rest of the race catching up. Miles was so fast, he was the only car the crowd watched. At the end, he did catch Davy, but didn't pass.

I started at Shelby American as the janitor. After the company started up, Ken would drop by regularly. After he came to work, he became the team manager. Even though I was the lowliest employee, Ken knew that I had just started to race my own car at an amateur level. I had purchased a Lotus Super 7 and I was getting ready to race it and Ken told me that he had a camshaft out of a Dolphin Formula Junior that Kurt Newman had driven (Ken had been a Dolphin factory driver). I'm not sure why he ended up with this cam, but he said, "Put it in your engine; it will help." I did and it really did help. It was the cam I always used in the car and I was quite successful in it. Ken's cam really brought it to life.

Later, every now and then Ken or Shelby would threaten to let me drive a car. It finally did happen at Sebring in 1964 when I co-drove with Ken. The interesting thing was that I had driven from California to Sebring in a Volkswagen Karmen Gia with two friends. Shelby had given us $25 each for travel expenses. Our job at Sebring was to be night watchmen. We drove non-stop from Venice to Florida. When we arrived, I saw Ken at tech inspection and he asked me if I had an FIA license. Of course, I didn't. The only thing I had was my SCCA license. I had lost my logbook. Ken asked if I could get one. I answered I didn't know how. I asked why I needed one and he said

that we might want you to become another team driver and drive with me in the 427 Cobra. He scribbled a note which said that John Morton was capable of driving and should be issued an FIA license. And signed it, "Ken Miles." I took the note to race headquarters at the old Kenilworth Hotel. So lo and behold, they gave me an FIA license.

When practice started, Ken crashed the car against a tree. When we got it back to the pits, it didn't look as if the car would even run. We beat the aluminum back into some sort of shape, but Al Doud wouldn't let me practice. Not including me, there were nine drivers for five cars. Al assumed that some of the cars would not last and he would switch drivers around. But none dropped out and Ken was getting tired. So in desperation, they stuck me in the car so Ken could rest. I drove it until the engine blew just before dark. That was my first racing experience with Ken.

After that, I traveled with the team quite a bit because I had purchased a Lotus 23 and Shelby would enter it for me as one of his Shelby-American factory cars. It went along with the other cars in the transporter. Ken was in incredible physical condition. At different race venues, I used to run with him. At that time by race driver standards, he was an old man (47). He was slender and even frail looking, but actually very tough. He could drive all day without relief. I was the only guy who would run with him in the morning. The others thought he was nuts. At five or six in the morning, he would bang on my door and off we would go.

I remember one time at Watkins Glen it was a very hot day. Ken won a 100-mile GT race in a Cobra. Then he ran the same car with a larger gas tank installed in the USRRC Championship event. I was in my Lotus 23. The race was about 180 miles. After the race, I was exhausted. "Aren't you tired?" I asked Ken. After all, he had driven these two races back to back in a Cobra, which takes a lot more strength than a Lotus. He chuckled, "No, not really." At that point, I decided I had a long way to go, and so did everyone else. I have never known another driver who had the kind of endurance Ken had.

Ken had a funny driving style. He would hold the steering wheel so delicately. And here he was driving cars (Cobras) that were just the opposite of delicate. I always recall the way he would grip the wheel using the sensitivity of his fingertips. Even though Miles was considerably older than the others of us, he didn't have any fear.

When he started driving the GT40s, I remember some really scary spins he had at Daytona. But they didn't seem to faze him. I thought, a guy that old (I was in my early twenties then) shouldn't be so casual about making mistakes.

Ken never seemed to be interested in driving the King Cobras (Cooper Monacos with a Ford V8). The weekend after Dave MacDonald was killed at Indy in 1964, we went to Mosport. We took a King Cobra that Dave was slated to drive plus a 289 Cobra and my Lotus. Obviously there was no driver for the King Cobra. Ken was offered the drive and he turned it down. He said he would rather drive the 289. At the last minute, Augie Pabst drove it and finished second to Bruce McLaren. Ken had just passed me in my Lotus when the tail shaft in the Cobra broke so he didn't finish.

Just before that Mosport event, I had taken delivery of my Lotus 23 that I had bought from Bob Challman in Manhattan Beach. Ken was going to Riverside to test a Cobra, so I took the Lotus along. I had never driven a rear-engine car before and it was spooky. I was intimidated and unsure of myself. So I asked Ken to take a few laps and check it out. He told me the car was fine and this gave me the confidence I needed to race the car.

The team went to Europe and didn't take me along. The last time I saw Ken was at Watkins Glen in 1966. He had just "lost" the race at Le Mans. He was extremely angry and incensed. He entered the Glen race in Otto Zipper's Porsche, but the engine blew in practice.

Shortly afterwards, Ken was killed testing the J-Car. I was working at Nickey Chevrolet and Charlie Hayes told me what had happened. It was hard to believe.

From my point of view, Ken had a rather odd personality. Some days he would be extremely friendly, talkative and helpful. Then there were other days when he would virtually ignore me. I could never get to know him well enough to call him a close friend. But I would like to have and I had a tremendous amount of respect for him

AUGIE PABST REMEMBERS

I met Ken about 1959 when the Meister Brauers entered the L.A. Times GP at Riverside. I was driving a Scarab and Lance Reventlow introduced us; Ken designed the initial layout of the Scarab chassis.

I was involved with Lance Reventlow and raced a Scarab, a car that I still own and use occasionally in vintage events.

I was at Mosport for the U.S. Road Racing Championship in June 8, 1964, scheduled to drive a Lola for John Mecom, Jr. We had problems with the car and I didn't even get it going to qualify.

The Shelby American team was there with Ken in charge. Their plan was to run not only production Cobras but also a King Cobra, a Cooper Monaco with a Ford engine. Dave MacDonald was scheduled to drive the Cooper, but unfortunately he had been killed at Indianapolis during the 500 the week before.

Ken saw that I was without a ride and asked me if I would be willing to drive the King Cobra if it was all right with Carroll. I said let me ask John Mecum and he said okay. Ken telephoned Carroll who also agreed.

I got in the car for practice. I came in and said that I hate to complain, but there's something wrong; the rear end is moving around coming up the main straight. Please check the rear toe-in. Sure enough, it was too far out. They fixed the problem and the car was terrific.

I ended up second overall. As I went around, I noticed Ken at the side of the road. On the cool-off lap, I stopped and picked him up. After he was in the seat of the Cooper, I tried to scare him.

Ken Miles always seemed to me to be the same. He never appeared to be upset or angry. He just took things the way they were. If there was a problem, he would sort it out. I appreciated him letting me drive the car. It handled really well and went pretty damn fast. I had previously driven a Cooper Monaco with the small Buick V8 engine for Briggs Cunningham. It didn't have nearly enough power. In those days, the tires were really narrow. It wasn't like today; we didn't have the down force. But to me, the cars of that day were much more fun to drive. Racing back in those days was a hell of a lot more fun.

They gave me a check for placing second, but I don't remember the exact amount. I do remember that I bought a window air conditioner for my house with the money.

From then on, every time I turned on the air conditioner, I thought of Mosport and Ken Miles. He had a neat sense of humor; he was very special.

Augie Pabst drove this King Cobra for Shelby American on June 6, 1964 at Mosport in the U.S. Road Racing Championship event placing second overall. The engine on Ken Miles' Cobra had blown, so Ken was at the side of the road. Augie stopped to pick up Miles on the cool-off lap and drove Ken back to the paddock.

During the Cobra years, Shelby entered his team members in both series of the U.S. Road Racing Championship. One, the Manufacturer's Championship, was for production cars; the other was for Driver's, usually in sports racing cars. Here, Miles competes at Riverside on April 26, 1964. *Photo: Harold Treichler*

Ken Miles won the April 26, 1964 USRRC Manufacturer's race at Riverside. Starter Arnie Cane leans over Ken to congratulate him as Race Queen Marilyn Fox (later Lothar Motschenbacher's wife) approaches. Carroll Shelby's Cobras won the Manufacturer's series that year with Ken leading the team. *Photo: Allen Kuhn*

Ken Miles in the Shelby Cobra with Shelby's personal racing number at Road America in September 1964. That year was one of triumph for Shelby and Miles. Ken won the USRRC Manufacturer's Championship for the team with first places in March at Augusta and Sebring, April at Pensacola, May at Kent, June at Watkins Glen, July at Greenwood, August at Meadowdale, and September at Road America and Bridgehampton! *Photo by Ray Boldt*

The competition was tough and the fields were filled in the USRRC Manufacturer's Championship series. Ken Miles (#98, far right) leads the field from the pole on the first lap at Laguna Seca in May 1965. Ed Leslie is second in #96. Leslie ended up first overall with Ken second and Bob Johnson third in another Cobra.

The Shelby American team celebrates their victory at the 1965 Daytona. Ken Miles (left) has his arm around Carroll Shelby, Lloyd Ruby (kneeling), Leo Beebe and Ray Geddes.

Miles and Ruby were first overall in a Ford GT-40 at the Daytona Continental 2000 km Race on February 28, 1965. Ray Geddes was the Ford Sports Car Manager; Leo Beebe was Manager, Special Vehicles Department. The Shelby-American team took the first four places overall with Jo Schlesser and Hal Keck second in a Daytona Coupe, Bob Bondurant and Richie Ginther third in another GT-40 and John Timanus and Rick Muther fourth in another Daytona. Ken Miles was the Competition Manager for Shelby, demonstrating complete domination of the 1965 Daytona.

At Sebring, Miles and Bruce McLaren were second in a GT-40 (next page), and at Monza in April they were third. At Riverside, Ken was second in a Cobra and he won in a Cobra at Laguna Seca.

Ken conferring with Bruce McLaren seated in the GT40 at Sebring.

Ken failed to finish at Le Mans in 1965.

At the 12-Hours of Sebring, Carroll Shelby paired Miles with Bruce McLaren in the Ford. They finished second overall and first in the prototype category. In the photo below, Ken leaps out of the GT40 for a driver change during a gas stop. All photos on these pages are by Dave Friedman, the official Shelby American team photographer.

Above: Team Manager Carroll Smith consults with Miles during a pit stop. Below: When night fell, it rained and the track was flooded. Ken's expertise driving in the rain undoubtedly contributed greatly.

1966 was the year of Ken's greatest triumphs and, of course, the unspeakable tragedy. The year started off with a bang. Ken and Lloyd Ruby won the Daytona Continental 24-Hour on February 5-6 for Ford and Shelby American in a GT40. Technically, the car was a MK IIB.

The event was a triumphant sweep for Shelby too. GT40s finished first, second and third. Dan Gurney and Jerry Grant were second with Walt Hansgen and Mark Donahue third. Bruce McLaren and Chris Amon were fifth in another Shelby Ford.

At Sebring on March 26, Miles and Ruby won again, this time in a Ford GT40 X-1. This was a roadster originally driven without success by Bruce McLaren. It was brought to Shelby American and refitted with a MK II rear body section, a new shorter nose and a different windscreen. Hansgen and Donahue took second, but it was a Hollman & Moody GT40 rather than a Shelby American. The victory might have been Dan Gurney's and Jerry Grant's. They led the event for almost the entire distance, but their car broke down only a half mile from the finish line at the end of the race.

The photographs on this page were taken at Sebring while that on the opposing page was taken at Daytona. The one at the right shows Ken and Lloyd Ruby accepting cup from the trophy girl.

The winners of the 1966 24-Hours of Daytona: Lloyd Ruby (left) and Ken Miles (holding trophy). Shelby American took all three top spots with Ford GT40s. Carroll Smith, Shelby team manager (wearing a cowboy hat), is behind and just to the right of Ruby.

The start of the 1966 Le Mans: Running at the right towards Ford MkII number 3 is Dan Gurney. Next to him running towards the number 1 MkII is Ken Miles. At the bottom right corner is Henry Ford II, running with the starter to get out of the way. Third in line is Sir John Whitmore who was teamed with Australian Frank Gardner to drive an Alan Mann entered MkII. Gurney, with co-driver Jerry Grant and Miles with co-driver Denny Hulme were Shelby American entries. Pedro Rodriguez, next to Sir John, is running towards the Ferrari P3. Graham Hill in the striped helmet is running towards another Alan Mann MkII. As it turned out, the first car away was the number 7 MkII driven by Graham Hill.
Photo courtesy L'Automobile Club de l'Ouest

From the start, Graham Hill led the pack for the first three laps when Dan Gurney passed into the lead, which he held for the first hour of the race. Then it began to rain and the pits were filled with cars changing tires.

For the next five hours, Gurney/Grant or Miles/Hulme in MkIIs led the way. At 10 p.m., the Rodriguez-Ginther Ferrari went in front, but only briefly. From then on, it was Ford MkIIs all the way. When the sun came up on Sunday morning, the first four were MkIIs. But then the Gurney-Grant car blew its head gasket, lost all its water and had to retire. This left three.

As the race drew to a close, it became obvious that Ford would win. Ken Miles and Denny Hulme had led most of the race and during the final minutes, they were ahead. Seeing that their cars would win, the Ford brass (read Henry II) decided that they would get the most publicity value from the race if all three Fords finished in a dead heat. Even though the race stewards had initially agreed to this scenario, after checking the rulebook, they advised Ford that a dead heat would be impossible.

The rules stated that the car that covered the most distance would be the winner. If, for example, two cars crossed the finish line in a dead heat, the car that was lined up the farthest from the start line would be the winner, having covered the most distance.

If Ford had not insisted on an attempt at a dead heat, Miles-Hulme would have won with Bruce McLaren and Chris Amon second with the Ronnie Bucknum/Dick Hutcherson Holman Moody MkII about 60 miles behind the leaders in third.

When the drivers came in for their last pit stop, they were informed of the dead heat decision. Ken Miles objected that the plan was unfair to Hulme and him, but he did agree to follow orders.

Paul Hawkins, another MkII driver who had to retire early on, tried to explain to the Ford people that under Le Mans rules, a dead heat was impossible. They chose to ignore Hawkins, but finally an official informed them, but by then it was too late and the cars were on their last lap. Miles had slowed way down so the other two could catch up.

If Miles and McLaren had crossed in a dead heat, McLaren would have been declared the winner because, due to qualifying times, the Miles-Hulme car was lined up ahead of the McLaren-Amon one. But that's not what happened.

Bruce McLaren (left) about to cross the finish line ahead of Ken Miles (right) with the Bucknum/Hutcherson MkII behind Miles.

Miles knew the rules and knew McLaren would win if the two were in a dead heat. As the cars approached the finish line on their final lap, Ken purposely slowed down and allowed Bruce to cross ahead. He was angry with the Ford gurus and became rather disconsolate. Winning the world's most prestigious sports car race would have been a real crown to his career.

In those days, Le Mans, the 24-Hours of Daytona and the 12-Hours of Sebring were known as the triple crown of sports car racing. Miles had already won Daytona and Sebring that year. And he would have won that triple crown but for…

I had dinner with Ken and Mollie two months later and he seemed resigned to accepting the unacceptable results. He was looking forward to bigger and better things and was convinced that his driving career had not yet peaked. But as it turned out of course, it was not to be.

34èmes Grand Prix d´Endurance les 24 Heures du Mans 1966

Circuit de la Sarthe

Date:	June 18-19, warm, dry, drizzles on sunday	**Track Length (m):**	13 461
Attendance:	350 000	**Pole Position:**	Dan Gurney, USA, Ford GT Mk II, 3'30"6 = 230.103 km/h
Entries:		**Fastest Lap:**	Dan Gurney, USA Ford GT Mk II, 3'30"6 = 230.103 km/h
Practiced:	57	**Distance (km):**	4843.090
Starters:	55	**Average Speed (km/h):**	210.795
Classified:	15		

Pos	Classific.	#	Team / Entrant Car - Engine	Drivers, Nationality	Engine Vol (cc)	Engine Type	Group	Laps Km Hour	Reason Out/ Notes
1	1	2	Shelby American Inc., USA Ford GT40 Mk II	Bruce McLaren, NZ Chris Amon, NZ *DNS Bob Grossmann, USA DNS Dan Gurney, USA*	6982	V8	P	4843.090 360	
2	2	1	Shelby American Inc., USA Ford GT40 Mk II	Ken Miles, GB/USA Denis Hulme, NZ *DNS Lloyd Ruby, USA DNS Lucien Bianchi. B*	6982	V8	P	4843.070 360	
3	3	5	Holman & Moody, USA (Essex Wire Corporation, USA) Ford GT40 Mk II	*DNS Richard Thompson, USA DNS Mark Donohue, USA* Ronnie Bucknum, USA Richard 'Dick' Hutcherson, USA *DNS A.J. Foyt, USA DNS Fred Lorenzen, USA DNS Bob Grossman, USA DNS Bruce McLaren, NZ DNS Peter Arundell, GB*	6982	V8	P	4681.570 348	
4	4	30	Porsche System Engineering, D Porsche 906/6 Carrera 6 Langheck	Jo Siffert, CH Colin Davis, GB *DNS Gerhard Mitter, D*	1991	F6	P	4562.130 339	

This is the official Le Mans record of the 1966 event reproduced from their web site (http://user.tninet.se/~aiq291w/1966.htm). It shows the McLaren/Amon GT40 MkII traveling 0.020 kilometers farther than the Miles/Hulme car. In other words, the Le Mans officials scored McLaren as being 20 meters (65.57 feet) ahead of Miles. But the photograph on the previous page shows the three GT40s just before the finish line. It appears that the Miles car almost overlapped the rear of McLaren's. How can the official record be correct?

THE FINISH

Henry Manney in the September 1966 edition of *Road & Track* reported the race as follows:

The lead had varied back and forth through the night, mostly the property of Miles and Hulme, passed on to Gurney/Grant and then to McLaren/Amon before it went back to Gurney…and then his red No. 3 came to a shuddering halt far too hot for the engine's good.

The Fords dropped to slower than 4-min laps but keeping a wary eye on each other, Miles in the lead but McLaren and Bucknum not too far behind. At the last pit stops comp chief Beebe had a fairly serious talk with the boys with the result that Miles began to moderate his pace towards the end and as they crept around for the last lap, trying for a group finish if not actually a photo-finish 1-2-3. Miles was seen to slacken off appreciably and actually brake to let McLaren cross the line first.

It doesn't matter that there was a lot of curious comment in the French papers afterward about Miles and Hulme being almost dragged up onto the winner's podium first and then suddenly shoved aside for the New Zealanders McLaren and Amon. It doesn't matter about Miles being a bit choked, as why shouldn't he be, having driven a lot of the race in front and done a lot of the development work. It doesn't matter, although it is puzzling. It doesn't matter that an English pilot was heard to remark in jest (not Miles) that those flymin' Antipodeans shouldn't have been transported and why after all that trouble for an American win, Ford didn't have an American driver.

It's interesting to note that a chart included with the Manney article shows the McLaren/Amon and the Miles/Hume cars traveling the same distance at 3002.7.

I conducted a taped interview with Carroll Shelby on November 20, 2003. Carroll said, "What we decided was that all three of them (Miles, McLaren, Bucknum), would go over the finish line at the same time. That was a decision made by Leo Beebe and myself. It was passed by Mr. Ford (Henry II). There was never any thought that we didn't want Ken Miles to win. We slowed Ken up to let the others catch up. Ken was not asked to let McLaren win. We decided to have all three cars cross the finish line at the same time. The Le Mans officials made up a rule that said that the car that had traveled the farthest by ten feet would win. It was a rule that wasn't in the book. This is what cost Ken the race. I felt very bad about it. I felt very guilty because Ken did deserve to win. I felt worse about it after he was killed."

I remarked that a photograph shows McLaren ahead of Ken at the finish line. Carroll answered, "I know McLaren was ahead just before the finish line, but they were all damn close together when the flag dropped. They were so close that the Frenchman had to make a decision. The photograph shows them about 75 or 100 feet before the line. I don't believe Ken backed off to let McLaren get ahead."

Carroll Shelby portrait by Art Evans

Another eyewitness, Albert Bochroch in his *Americans at Le Mans* had this to say:

"To my eyes and to no less an authority than John Bond, the respected publisher of *Road & Track*, McLaren seemed to speed up for the last few yards, reaching the start-finish line a good car length in front of Ken Miles.

As the viewing angle of the finish line can be deceptive, those who differed from the official version had remained quiet. Only recently did Ken Miles' driving partner, Denny Hulme, settle the issue when he told me, 'There isn't any question about it. The starting position hassle was academic as Bruce speeded up at the very end and was a car length ahead of Ken at the finish.' Hulme recalls, 'Ken was very upset. We had led most of the race and we had to slow way down to let Chris and Bruce catch up. Ken just couldn't get over it.'

The Quote from *Road & Track* was used courtesy of Editor Tom Bryant. Quote from *Americans At Le Mans* was used courtesy of Publisher Walter R. Haessner of the Aztex Corporation.

KEN MILES, an appreciation

By James T. Crow

(Reprinted with permission from the November 1966 edition of *Road & Track*.)

The death of Ken Miles has created a unique sort of void in the lives of an uncommonly large number of people. Personally, I have known no other driver whose death has touched so many people in some private, special sort of way.

Ken was killed at Riverside Raceway on August 17 while testing one of the Ford J-car prototypes. The testing program that was being carried out was to determine whether the J-car was suited for participation in this fall's Canadian-American Championship series. A series of trouble-free laps had been made before the accident and on the final lap, there was nothing to indicate anything wrong as the car came down the backstretch at about 175 mph. Then, toward the end of the straight when the car had slowed to approximately 100, it went out of control, spun to the inside of the course and went over a tall embankment. The car bounded end over end and Ken, thrown out of the car, was dead of head injuries before emergency crews reached the scene. The main section of the chassis caught fire after coming to rest and the fire damage, plus the physical battering given the scattered components in the violent series of crashes, make it doubtful that the reason for the accident will ever be determined. It may not matter now, except for our own satisfaction, no one who knew Ken's driving can believe that the accident resulted from a mistake on his part.

The funeral was held the following Saturday and the chapel would not hold all the people who came to pay final respects to a man whose career was unique in the history of American racing.

Ken's early career has been documented in a number of biographical sketches and articles. Several of the better ones have appeared in Road & Track during the last ten years.

He was born in the city of Sutton Coldfield, England, a few miles from the manufacturing center of Birmingham, on November 1, 1918. Always intrigued by mechanical things, he was apprenticed to a British car manufacturer, but World War II intervened and he spent seven years on various duties having to do with machinery and mechanics and was a sergeant of tanks at his demobilization in 1946. After this, he returned to the motor industry in various jobs and continued a racing career that had been whetted by motorcycle racing while still in the service. His first racing car was a Frazer-Nash into which he inserted a Ford V8-60 engine and he enjoyed some small local successes in club events and hillclimbs. After an unsuccessful venture into building front-wheel drive F3 cars, he came to the U.S. in early 1952 as service manager for the Southern California MG distributor.

He first raced an MGTD in local road races, then began to attract widespread attention in his first MG Special. This car won the first race in which it participated (Pebble Beach 1953) and formed the basis for his being regarded as the finest under-1500cc car driver in the west. The original Miles special was a remarkably successful machine and because Ken made it look so easy, it was undoubtedly the inspiration for most of the homebuilt specials that appeared in California the next few years. As modern racing cars go, it was completely uncomplicated--front

engine, live rear axle, stock gearbox, almost no special components except chassis and body--and almost utterly reliable. As proof of the car's essential integrity, it was later campaigned by Cy Yedor, then by Dusty Miller and even after that by Dusty's son, Nels. And it was still a good car.

Next came the Flying Shingle, undoubtedly the most exciting special ever to appear in West Coast racing up till that time. It was lower, smaller, lighter and faster--but hardly more complicated--than the original MG Special. It ws not quite so successful as the first special, though Ken won more than his fair share of races in it. But times were changing and the cast-iron MG engine, even in racing tune, was being asked to do too much against the Porsches that were beginning to make their presence felt in racing then. But Ken and the Shingle were still the standard by which under-1500cc performance was measured. No one who was at the May 1956 Santa Barbara races will ever forget the racing between Miles in the Shingle and Pete Lovely in his then new Cooper-Porsche. Ken won on reliability, but Lovely's Pooper, demonstrably faster, was a sign of the times.

After the Shingle, which almost never raced again after Ken sold it and was last heard from when somebody tried to put half a Chevrolet V-8 in it, Ken began driving Porsche Spyders for Johnny von Neumann, the Southern California VW-Porsche distributor. I happened to be standing on the critical corner at Torrey Pines the first morning Ken drove a Spyder. It was for practice before the last or next-to-last Torrey Pines 6-hour races, and Ken kept coming through the left hand sweeper past the ocean turn faster and faster. We were still saying to each other, "Miles sure looks funny in a Porsche, doesn't he?" when Ken got off the road, hit a ditch and flipped spectacularly. The car landed on its wheels, Ken got out, looked at the battered car while stretching his back and accepted a ride back to the pits with, I think, Phil Hill. Ken didn't drive in the 6-hour race that Saturday, but on Sunday, in another von Neumann Spyder, he won the under-1500cc main event.

There was just one more Miles special, the Cooper-Porsche he built while working for von Neumann. This car, once sorted out (he was off the road almost more than on in the first race in that car), was so successful that Ken won over-1500cc main events with it and ultimately was forced to part with it because Porsche officials found it distasteful to have an employee in a special beating the factory's best products.

But after going to work for von Neumann, Ken became famous for the Porsches he drove, first for Johnny, later for Otto Zipper, and it was in Porsches that he reached the zenith of his career in smaller-engined cars. There was hardly a race in the west with any pretensions of importance in which Ken didn't drive a Porsche. And it seems to me that he lost only when his opponents had something newer.

The next large step came in Ken's career when he went to work for Carroll Shelby. He drove for Shelby before going to work for him full time, but it was after Ken became closely associated with Shelby American that his greatest national and international fame was achieved. No one who followed the first two seasons of the U.S. Road Racing Championship can forget Ken in the factory Cobra. It was in the Cobra that he finally and completely dispelled the myth that he could drive only small-engined cars and it was through Shelby American and the Cobra campaigns that the rest of the U.S. was exposed to both Ken's driving and his personality. And that experience enriched both of them, I think.

His last season, of course, was the season of his greatness with victories at the Daytona 24-hour, the Sebring 12-hour and except-for-a-fluke, the Le Mans 24-hour race. For these things alone, Ken's name will be remembered for a long time. And it is fitting that his name should be remembered, for his driving earned it.

Yet his racing record, even if it were to include every race he ever ran, couldn't do more than hint at what Ken Miles was like or what he meant to the sport. Nor have the biographical sketches. Nor the uniformly respectful obituaries that have appeared since his death.

No amount of cold factual information can convey how much Ken meant to the formative years of road racing in Southern California. For example, when I discovered road racing, Ken was the president of the California Sports Car Club and winning consistently in his first MG Special. He was not only the hero driver of the day, he also ran the club that staged the races. And furthermore, he built the car in which he won the under-1500cc races (which were an hour long in those days) and, in all likelihood, finished no worse than third or fourth in the over-1500cc races. To so many of us, he was road racing in those days.

Ken represented what road racing was all about. It was not only courage, which we had seen before in the traditional round-track racing, but it was also coolness, skill, finesse. Anybody could go fast on the straight--if he could afford the car that would do it--but it was Ken who showed us about going deeper into corners, who shifted down with immense skill and who would probably continue to smile as he passed an adversary on the inside. He had style and we loved it.

He exemplified road racing to us, the idol who reflected everything that was new and intriguing about the sport. The first quick-lift jack I ever saw was used on his Flying Shingle during the over-1500cc main event at Palm Springs. Quick-lift jacks are nothing at all to me anymore, but that first one (one motion and the rear of the car was up in the air and a pit crew member was whacking the hub spinner off a wire wheel), entering into a consciousness that had never previously known anything more glamorous than a garden-variety floor jack, was something pretty special.

And Ken knew about the organization of racing, too. He was the Cal Club and when he ran it, he ran it from a driver's point of view and for the driver's benefit. So he was not only a driver who could build a winning car, he also knew how to set up a circuit, how to arrange a starting grid and what the procedure should be for scrutineering.

In other words, we believed Ken Miles knew everything that needed to be known about road racing and we were properly respectful because we barely knew an Su from an Amal and a Weber was something we'd read about in *Road & Track*.

He talked and we listened and we learned. We watched and we admired. And his British accent, even if slightly incomprehensible as it came out of the side of his mouth, seemed exactly right.

Yes, we discovered Ken Miles when we discovered the marvelous new world of road racing and his name became part of our conversation along with such things as shut-off points, Mowog and heel-and-toe. His death is all the more poignant because it severs a link with that period of wonder and excitement.

But that isn't the whole Ken Miles either. In all I've written so far, there isn't a hint that Ken wasn't loved by everyone who knew him—and the fact that he wasn't was an essential part of Ken Miles too. Ken made enemies along the way and many of us can remember a time when hardly anyone could be found who had a good word to say about any Ken Miles except Ken Miles the driver.

When he ran the Cal Club, for instance, he ran it his way and without much consideration for the feelings or opinions of anyone else. He wanted things done his way, and he didn't want to discuss his decision with the non-racers either.

At the peak of his strength in the Cal Club, he fought the local SCCA region right down to the ground. He led other drivers in refusing to race in Los Angeles Region races and, for a good many years, seemed to enjoy baiting SCCA officials. He rather enjoyed the fact that his application for membership was refused by the SCCA even after he was no longer active in Cal Club affairs.

He was finally forced out of power in a palace revolution within the Cal Club and it was somehow ironically fitting and proper that years later, he was again a member of the Cal Club board of governors when the Los Angeles SCCA Regions was scuttled and the Cal Club became an SCCA Region.

Curiously, though, Ken was ruthlessly democratic in his own autocratic way of running the Cal Club. His leadership encouraged new drivers to race with the Cal Club when membership in most SCCA Regions was still based on the old-boy system and if you weren't the right type, you simply weren't put up for membership. Under Ken's leadership, the Cal Club had ten full-fledged race meets a year, real damned good road racing that didn't let the socializing interfere with the club's proper purpose. This intense racing program, which was largely Ken's creation, created an atmosphere that encouraged young drivers and the outstanding crop of Southern California drivers who got their start in those days (the list starts with Dan Gurney) owe more to Ken Miles than they generally realize.

It is unfortunate that Ken was never properly thanked for all he did for Southern California road racing. It is probably true, also, that he would have brushed it off had anyone tried.

There were still more sides to Ken Miles. He also had charm. Wit and charm like almost no one I've ever known. But if he could be elaborately polite, he also had a command of sarcasm that could make your teeth shrink. It's generally forgotten took that he could write and that some of the columns he did for *Competition Press* were superb.

While we're on the subject, it should be recorded too that not every step he took led upward, either. With his ability to alienate people who could have been helpful to him, he went through and past a lot of what could have been good jobs. It was said about him that he was his own worst enemy and this was undoubtedly true as he could have had almost anything he wanted if he could have been more tactful. Only in this last job--working for Shelby--did everything seem to be right. Ken never lost the sharp edge to his tongue, but he and Shelby had a rapport based on mutual respect and admiration.

Los Angeles Times

Ken Miles Killed in Riverside Crash

by Bob Thomas, Times Auto Editor
Thursday, August 18, 1966

One of road racing's best known and oldest active drivers is dead.

Ken Miles of Hollywood died late Wednesday in a violent crash of a Ford test race car at Riverside International Raceway.

The outspoken but popular 47-year-old driver apparently died instantly when the high-powered, low-slung sports car he was driving plunged off a high bank and bounced end-over-end several times into the infield.

Miles, according to witnesses, was thrown out of the car on the third revolution. The car on final impact burst into flames and was totally destroyed. Miles was not burned.

Officials were unable to determine the cause of the accident which occurred at the end of the track's mile-long back straightaway. It was estimated that he was traveling at 175 m.p.h. prior to breaking on the approach to the circuit's ninth and final turn, a sweeping, high-speed curve. The driver's son, 18-year-old Peter, was at the track at the time of the accident. Miles is also survived by his wife, Mollie.

Miles had been testing the machine, a prototype designated by Ford as the "J" car, for several days at the track. The car is a successor to the (GT40) Mark II model that recently won the Le Mans enduro classic in France and was being tested to evaluate its potential for a series of upcoming professional sports car races in North America.

It was reported unofficially that Miles broke the Riverside lap record of 1 minute, 26.4 seconds with it Tuesday.

The death of the colorful driver shocked his many friends and followers in the Southern California area where he has made his home for more than a decade.

During that period he won more races than any other western driver. He was always admired for his precise driving techniques and rarely was involved in accidents.

His death marked a tragic end to the greatest season Miles has enjoyed since he started racing in his native England in 1938. He had won two of the year's three major endurance sports car races--the Sebring 12-hour and Daytona 24-hour--and missed a "grand slam" only on a fluke when he was awarded second place at LeMans in June when a Ford Motor Co. attempt to stage a "photo-finish" with two of its cars backfired.

Since 1963, Miles had been the No. 1 team driver and chief test driver for Shelby American of Los Angeles, helping develop such famous sports cars as the Shelby Daytona Cobra, Mustang GT 350, Ford GT 40 and Mark II.

Carroll Shelby, president of Shelby American and long-time close friend of Miles, was in Detroit when the accident occurred and was unavailable for comment.

Dan Gurney, teammate or rival of Miles for many years, praised Miles for his "courage and dedication to the game."

"Ken certainly earned the victories that had come to him the last couple of years after the exposure he had in thousands of miles of the toughest kind of testing," said Gurney. "He had run cars in their experimental stages and yet never flinched in accepting such a big challenge, one that not many drivers are really ready to accept."

Gurney, incidentally, is scheduled to test his own Lola-Ford sports car at Riverside today.

Miles took a philosophical approach to the dangers of auto racing. "If you are going to indulge in the sport, that's one of the things you have to face . . . and accept," he said recently.

The slender and wiry veteran, whose tongue could be as sharp as his cockney accent when it came to facing controversial issues, was noted for his keen attention to physical fitness. It contributed no doubt to his remarkable performances in endurance races and ability to match talents with the world's best drivers at an age when most athletes have retired.

He teamed with Texan Lloyd Ruby to win the 24-hour Daytona race in February and the 12-hour Sebring enduro in March. He was leading at Le Mans on his way to an unprecedented "sweep" when Ford made its decision to dramatize the victory with a deadheat involving Miles and his teammate, Dennis Hulme, and New Zealanders Bruce McLaren and Chris Amon. It didn't come off.

A former British army sergeant, Miles drove motorcycles and sports cars in England before coming to the United States in 1952.

Miles, who became a naturalized American citizen, began racing on the West Coast with the California Sports Car Club and later became one of the country's top Porsche drivers, setting a record of 49 finishes in 49 starts, most of them victories, while teamed with car owner Otto Zipper of Beverly Hills.

Later, he carried Shelby American to the U.S. manufacturers championship by winning the national driving title and contributed to Shelby's Subsequent world championship.

Funeral services are pending at Utter-McKinley Hollywood Mortuary.

Ford Will Probe Death-Car Crash

by Bob Thomas, Times Auto Editor
August 19, 1966

Mechanical failure apparently triggered the high-speed crash at Riverside International Raceway Wednesday that took the life of race driver Ken Miles of Hollywood.

Miles was testing a new prototype GT (Grand Touring) sports car developed by Ford Motor Co. when the accident occurred.

President Carroll Shelby of Shelby American, which was conducting the test program for Ford, said Thursday, "We really don't know what caused it. The car just disintegrated."

Shelby, badly shaken by the loss of his No. 1 test driver and long-time friend, said an investigation would be held in an attempt to determine the cause.

A member of his staff speculated that "something locked up" in the car, presumably brakes or the power-train, throwing it out of control.

An eye-witness account, describing the cars' behavior before it plunged off a steep bank at the end of the track's mile-long straight, supported this theory.

Extensive damage to the car, however, may block efforts to determine the exact cause. The car burned upon impact. Miles was thrown clear but died instantly from massive head and internal injuries.

Funeral services for the 47-year-old driver will be held Saturday at 2.30 p.m. in Utter-McKinley Wilshire Mortuary, 444 S. Vermont, with cremation and inurnment to follow at Hollywood Memorial Park Mausoleum, 6,000 Santa Monica Blvd.

Track observer and fireman Jud Weirbach, who was stationed at the end of the straight, said there was no indication of trouble when Miles came down the back stretch, approaching the final turn, at a speed estimated at 180 m.p.h. "He was following a normal line," said Weirbach. "He shut off at the usual spot and slowed to somewhere near 100 m.p.h.

It was at that point, said Weirbach, that the rear end of the car suddenly veered to the left. "As Miles corrected, the rear come around to the right and got into the dirt on the edge of the track. The car was almost broadside when it left the track."

The car is one of two J-category prototypes built by Ford as a possible successor to the Mark II which won the Le Mans endurance classic in France two months ago. It was fully instrumented and was being evaluated for possible entry in professional sports car races and, depending on the rules, for next year's Le Mans event. One of its innovations was an automatic transmission.

Shelby, who was in Detroit when the crash occurred, returned to Los Angeles immediately. He described the veteran driver, whose career spanned nearly 30 years, as the "greatest test driver in the world."

"We have nobody to take his place. There is nobody," said the saddened Shelby, who credited Miles with a major role in the development of the world championship-winning Cobra sports car, the Shelby Mustang GT 350 as well as the Ford GT 40 and Mark II cars.

"He was our baseline, our guiding point," added Shelby. "He was the backbone of our program . . . the guy who rode shotgun for us when things were tough."

Miles won the Sebring 12-hour and Daytona 24-hour in Florida this year and missed a sweep of the world's three major endurance events when a technicality deprived him of a victory at Le Mans.

Miles, who left his native England in 1952 to become an American citizen, leaves his wife, Mollie, and son, Peter, 18. Young Miles was at the track when his father was killed.

Last Respects Paid to Miles
Sunday, August 21, 1966

More than 400 persons overflowed the Utter-McKinley Wilshire Chapel to pay their final respects Saturday to race car driver Ken Miles, who lost his life in a Riverside Raceway accident Wednesday.

Arthur W. Evans, a family friend, eulogized Miles as a man who loved auto racing, but who was also a devoted family man. Evans traced Miles life from his start in racing on a borrowed motorcycle, touching on things Ken was most remembered for but which are not found in record books.

Among the many racing personalities were Carroll Shelby and Otto Zipper, men who owned the cars Miles drove most of his racing career, as well as drivers Dan Gurney, Ronnie Bucknum, Skip Hudson, George Follmer, Scooter Patrick, Dave Jordan and Jerry Titus.

Ken Miles: The Victor Belongs to the Spoils
by Jack Smith

Ken Miles, a man who chose to drive fast cars for a living, took a turn too fast the other day and killed himself. Or maybe he didn't take the turn too fast. Maybe something went wrong with the car.

Miles was a prudent man, and not inclined to take turns too fast, though he was going 175 m.p.h., it is said, when he spun out at Riverside, overturned several times, and died.

Miles believed in traveling as fast as you can in this life without losing control, breaking up, spinning out and getting killed.

He spent his life close to the edge, and finally he went over it.

We don't have to feel sorry for people who choose to live dangerously, and lose. So the bull wins one. The matador must take the risk. The closer he plays to the horn, the better the show.

The late Ernest Hemmingway wrote two or three books and several magazine articles trying to explain that there is beauty in danger when it is deliberately sought out.

I met Miles once, at a cocktail party at the British consul general's home. It was, as you might imagine, an elegant affair. The Queen's servants are expected to act with dignity and grace at whatever expense.

Mr. Miles, I learned, was a man who handled a Scotch and soda with the same delicacy and precision he used in turning a car around the Riverside track. Not too fast, not to slow.

Miles was a tall, stringy, tough, intense, taciturn and absolutely courageous Englishman--not an unusual breed.

There were some British movie stars at the party. Rex Harrison? No, I don't believe he was there. Greer Garson? No, not Greer. Noel Coward? No, But there were some.

But it was Miles who captivated me. The movie stars had their little groups of admirers, but Miles had me and several others who wondered about this man whose life was dedicated to speed.

He had a bit of a Cockney accent, I suppose you would call it. He was without pretense. He was exquisitely polite.

I wouldn't want to misquote him. I wouldn't want to misquote anyone. But I did ask him, I believe, whether I could ever learn to be a racing driver.

He studied me carefully, looking mostly into my eyes as if the whole answer could be found there. Then he said, about, as I remember:

"That's up to you, sir, isn't it?"

A sound and generous answer. It was up to me, of course, and I decided against it. I don't believe I would have enough aplomb on the curves, or enough heart on the straightaways.

However, it was pleasant having a Scotch and soda with Miles, and being looked in the eye by him. I know, of course, he was warning me, in his polite way. Miles was a perfectionist. He would have advised anyone not as good as he was to stay out.

Race car driving is only for Miles and Stirling Moss, who had the sense to quit, and some of the others, who didn't.

Well, Miles, good show.

Le Mans Race Tribute to Miles
by Bob Thomas, Times Auto Editor

It's time to shed a tear again for an old friend. Ken Miles wouldn't want it that way. Tears aren't in order, he would say.

"Racing is a risky business," he told us last July. "I don't want to die, naturally, but if a man is going to drive race cars he has to accept the fact that it bloody well can happen." And it did to him. In August.

It was violent--while testing at Riverside Raceway--and, mercifully, quick.

At least it happened while he was doing what he liked to do best and at what he did best. If that's consolation, few men are so rewarded.

Then, why the tears today? Because Saturday they are running a race in Ken's memory . . . the 24-hours of Le Mans in France, the world's most famous endurance test of men and machinery.

Miles never won Le Mans. But he should have. No man ever came closer and didn't. By all rights, he should have taken that trophy with him to his grave.

After all, he was leading the race comfortably in its waning moments last year when a decision was made in this hour of triumph by Ford Motor Co. to

stage a dramatic deadheat with its two front-running cars.

But, of course, the best laid plans often go astray, which meant this hastily conceived bit of showmanship was doomed. And, in the theatrical avalanche of a 1-2-3 Ford finish, a technicality deprived Miles' car of the victory.

Also spoiled was his triple crown. He would have accomplished the unprecedented feat in 1966 of winning auto racing's three major endurance tests at Daytona, Sebring and finally Le Mans.

Miles came home shrouded in bitter disappointment. He was not one to bury his feelings. But, after expressing them, he said:

"Robert, please be careful how you report what I have said. I work for these people. They have been awfully good to me."

And he told them. In fact, if Ford repeats at Le Mans this year, Miles again will have played a part in the victory.

Ford hasn't forgotten. In an elaborate press kit prepared to outline its massive assault on the 1967 renewal of the classic Saturday, no attempt has been made to gloss lightly over the fact that Miles died tragically while testing the car Ford was preparing for this year's race.

It was the celebrated and ill-fated J-car, a problem child from the outset. Due to difficulties, it missed an appointment in 1966 at Le Mans. Luckily, its predecessor, the Ford GT Mark II, scored a "sweep" over the long-dominant Ferrari.

What caused Miles and the J-car to veer off course at high speed at the end of the Riverside straight last August remains a mystery.

Whatever it was, no one has suggested that Miles was an instrument of his own death. The precise driving Englishman with his incisive and heavily accented tongue was not a man known to miscalculations in a race car.

"There will never ever be another Ken Miles," said Carroll Shelby about his test driver-friend, dispelling any thought that those in the project felt Ken had erred.

Further troubles plagued the J-car. Without it, Ford's updated Mark IIs took a terrible shellacking

from revenge-bent Ferrari in February in the Daytona 24-hour.

Rechristened the Mark IV, the J-car finally made its long delayed debut at Sebring. Chassis problems were sorted out. And a new body shell, hastily designed by Phil Remington of Shelby American in Los Angeles, overcame seemingly everlasting aerodynamic difficulties.

Sebring ended in triumph. But it was a hollow conquest at best. Ferrari was not there.

Now the real showdown has arrived. With the J-car ready at last, Ford has prepared four of them among its six-car factory entry (plus two revised Mark IIs) for Saturday's big engagement with Ferrari at Le Mans.

We can only guess that Ken Miles will be there. It's a shame he won't be in the driver's seat.

But the sport can take refuge again behind an old phrase to cover his absence. Even Miles used it. It goes: "That's racing."

So Ken, we're sorry about the tears.

(Note: the preceding news stories from the archives of the *Los Angeles Times* were supplied by Motor Sports Editor Shav Glick.)

A personal note

Ken's death was a tragedy not only for his family and everyone in the racing world, but also very particularly for my family and me. My dad and Ken were best friends as were my stepmother, Betsy, and Mollie. The Miles' son, Peter, was friends with my younger siblings, especially my sister, April.

Until 1955 when I graduated, I was going to college on the GI Bill. I happened to take a course in journalism as an elective. While in that class, I met another sports car nut, Dick Sherwin, who became my best friend and partner. In order to get two extra units, Dick and I started a little magazine, the *West Coast Sports Car Journal*, later just the *Sports Car Journal*. While covering races, I met Ken and we became friends. He sort of took me under his wing and he was my hero, even though he was a terror on public highways.

From time to time, Ken, Mollie, my current sweet-heart and I would have dinner together. Our favorite restaurant was the old Captain's Table on La Cienega. In 1958, we arranged for a dinner and Ken asked me to bring my Devin SS demonstrator as he had not yet seen it. After dinner, we decided to go to the Miles home on Sunday Trail for a drink. My date was Linda Valentine, a former Rose Princess and daughter of an SCCA official. Ken wanted to drive the Devin, so he and Linda went in the Devin while Mollie and I followed in Ken's beater. Sunday Trail is high in the Hollywood Hills and you get there on small, winding roads, often with water running off lawn sprinklers and cars parked every which way. When Millie and I arrived, I found a shaken Linda and a damp Devin passenger seat.

After I graduated, the Draft Board decided, in error, to call me up. I didn't know how to protest, so I showed up for the physical. When I took my clothes off, they noticed my dog tags and eventually discovered their mistake. In the meantime, my dad had volunteered to help Dick with the magazine. Ken was a contributor; he and my dad became very close.

Somehow their personalities seemed to mesh, not necessarily a usual thing for Ken. My folks had a ranch in the Newhall area of Los Angeles County and the Miles family spent a great deal of free time there. My dad had a 1927 Pirsch fire engine. He used to say that he went to fires only by appointment. The ranch had a meandering dirt

Ken and my father, Art Evans, Sr., in 1958.

road that made a circuit. With Evans children and Peter aboard, Ken used to try to better his lap times in the Pirsch.

In 1966, I was living at Mary Davis' Portofino Inn in Redondo Beach. Ken had just won Daytona, Sebring and, almost, Le Mans. He and Mollie came down to have dinner with me and my date. I recall that Mary stopped by to say hi and others wanted autographs.

A week or so later, I was in Mexico City on a photo assignment. My dad called me at my hotel at four in the morning to tell me that Ken had been killed. Mollie insisted that dad deliver the eulogy and we talked about what he would say. Unfortunately, I couldn't get back in time for the service.

After we hung up, the tears came . . .

AFTERMATH

A few days after that first call to my hotel room in the Maria Isabel Hotel in Mexico City, my dad called again to discuss what he would say at the service. I know that my father always typed a speech prior to its delivery. I was sure that he had done so for that occasion. When I started this scrapbook project, I wanted to include the eulogy. So I went over all of my father's effects looking for the manuscript. But try as I could, neither my brother, Robb, nor I could find it. We decided that it just wasn't going to turn up.

When I visited Peter Miles, he had promised to share his photograph and memorabilia collection. He had a large box full to the brim. Lo and behold, he found the eulogy near the bottom. It is a now-faded carbon copy and somewhat difficult to decipher. So rather than reproducing it, I re-typed it.

EULOGY BY ART EVANS, SR.

We are here today to honor Kenneth Miles and to reassure his wife, Mollie, and his son, Peter, of our continued devotion. Mollie has asked me to express her deep gratitude for your many kindnesses.

Would that I could manipulate words with that same degree of nice parsimony that was Ken's outstanding attribute as a driver. But words, at best, are such fearfully inadequate vehicles in which to express the feelings that are in our hearts.

Today, our thoughts of Ken Miles are of the rich memories he has given us. All of us who knew Ken will treasure those memories. Throughout the racing world, whenever and wherever enthusiasts gather for that time-honored ritual of bench racing, the name of Ken Miles will be heard. In the years to come, his name will be remembered as it has been increasingly heard ever since his first fearful experiment with speed on a borrowed motorcycle years ago in his native England.

Each of us will travel back over our own many trails. They may well be vastly different from Ken's. For he was a complex man with a keen, incisive intelligence and an insatiable desire for knowledge. The worlds of music, literature and art were as familiar to Ken as was the machinery that he loved. The result is that we, his friends, have widely varied memories. Ken Miles was a vivid man.

Ken knew no such thing as half-heartedness. His tremendous enthusiasm for any new experience never waned; his zest for living never paled. The record books will show that Ken's greatest interest and his finest achievements were in the development and driving fine racing machinery. The automotive world, on and off the track, is far richer today because of the contributions that Ken has made to it. These contributions were made possible because of his hard-earned knowledge, his inherent skill and, above all, his enthusiasm for his chosen profession and sport.

I am sure that today, as each of us travel back over our own private memory trails, that our thoughts will not dwell on Ken's achievements as a superlative driver. For that, record books will suffice. Our thoughts, rather, will turn to other things, the sort of things that you don't put into record books. Memories that are too vivid to record and too varied to catalog.

How can any of us forget the story of that brash young man who had the temerity to ask a very beautiful girl on their first date to ride in a mechanized monstrosity spewing oil and petrol, to say nothing of assorted but vital parts, over a quiet English countryside. A machine that proved a master for the budding Miles mechanical genius and left the devoted couple afoot far from her doorstep. If you can overlook, after such an episode, that persistent young man's confounded audacity in asking the girl to marry him. How can we but admire his success!

That was the first, and by far the most important victory in Ken's long record. And those of us who have been privileged to know Ken, Mollie and Peter during the intervening years know that, even then, Ken demonstrated his unique ability for outrageous audacity coupled with good judgment.

Ken was an enthusiast and proud of it. When war came to England, of course he joined his countrymen and put to good use his growing knowledge of machinery, his skill and enthusiasm. Stories from those war years indicate there is some possibility Ken was quite as devastating as the tanks, which he drove. Ken and Mollie were married during that war. Then, as in all of the years since, Mollie was at her husband's side, meeting with quiet humor and infinite patience the triumphs and hazards of Ken's unquenchable spirit.

Ken loved his native England. Make no mistake about that. But when he and Mollie came to the United States and to Hollywood, he entered into the life of his new country with enthusiasm. One of Ken's greatest achievements and one of his greatest successes was to become a good as well as a legal citizen of his adopted land. An indication of this is in Ken's deep concern for the plight of our American Indians. Much as he detested sham and hypocrisy, he had a high regard for history and tradition. He valued the deep roots which his own family has in English history and he found it difficult to understand how we in this country could so neglect our own rich Indian heritage.

Of course Ken was British. His use of words made that identification unmistakable. Ken used the English language with the same precision that was his trademark as a driver. But his was not a Cockney accent and those who have suggested it betrayed their own lack of knowledge of English as it should be used . . . as Ken Miles used it.

Many will remember that just this year at Daytona, as the race neared the finish, Ken was leading the pack. His margin was enough to persuade him that he should stop in the pits for a quick shower and change of clothing. All would have gone well except that when he attempted to return to the track, the guards failed to recognize him and, had it not been for the timely appearance of his close friend and co-worker, Carroll Shelby, the winning car would have been without one of its drivers.

Ken had no use for meaningless pomp and there are those who will remember an occasion when he and his crew, in search of dinner, found themselves in a restaurant where they were refused admittance because of their lack of ties. Ken's solution to this pretty problem was direct and effective. He and his friends removed their shoelaces, and from them devised ties that may have been unusual, but met the immediate need.

There are other sorts of memories such as when Peter and his friend were told by their mothers that it was bedtime. The mothers were thwarted by the irrepressible father who considered romping with his son more important than sleep. And there is the memory of Ken wandering through a Pasadena garden displaying an unsuspected knowledge of plants and unadulterated admiration for their beauty. (Author's note: The garden was my father's mother-in-law's)

Ken and Mollie made their home high in the Hollywood Hills on as rugged a piece of California real estate as one could well hope to find. Many have memories of the little house when they first moved in and of that bare plot of ground. Those who have visited this home over the years will have more memories of how Ken's skill and his enthusiasm caused this modest cottage to grow into a charming and gracious home and the rocky hillside to become a beautiful garden.

There are so many bright memories, and they all contribute to the depth and the brilliance of the pattern that was Ken's life. But life, brilliant and vital as it may be, is an uncertain thing for everyone. It is in the memories of a life that we can find the immortal. And it is in the words of a poet that I have found my own enduring picture of Ken:

"He met with joy each fighting morn,
full throated, drinking deep of life."

PETER MILES REMEMBERS

My earliest memory of my dad was a time when he was driving the R-1. (1953; Peter was five years old.) My dad had won the race and I ran up along side the car to give him a hug. I burned my leg on the exhaust pipe and I remember crying and screaming; it hurt so bad. Another time at Riverside when I was about thirteen, I was making tea for him while he was out on the track in the Sunbeam Alpine. I was boiling water on one of those little propane stoves and I spilled it on my foot burning it rather badly.

What I remember most was helping him out at our home on Sunday Trail. He was always doing something in the yard. He had this old Fiat Multipla. We used to drive that thing up in the hills. My dad would find rocks and we would load the Multipla with all the rocks it could handle. We would bring them home and build retaining walls. My job was to help out and stop the rocks from rolling. My mom had a rose garden in the front.

When dad first went to work for Shelby, I was sixteen. He would bring home Cobras and GT350s that he was working on setting up for the street. He would take me down to the hobby shop in those cars.

Of course, everyone in the shop would come running out. He took me to the hobby shop because I used to race slot cars. Going home up the street to Sunday Trail was a lot of fun.

My dad took me out to Willow Springs in the first 427 Cobra. He was going out to do some testing. When we got there, he let me drive around the track with him in the passenger seat. I didn't think I was doing anything serious. But I got going so fast that I had to grab the seat and thought, whoa. So I slowed down a little bit.

I don't know how many times I went with him out to various tracks to race or for testing. I remember sitting and waiting in the car and being utterly bored. At Santa Barbara, I remember we always went to a restaurant named Carl's Steak House. It was always crowded and everyone was talking. That was boring too. I would fall asleep at the table. I don't know how many times we went there.

In the mornings, dad used to jog. He would carry one or two pound dumbbells in his hands. A few times, I would jog along with him. These days, I don't jog, but I like to hike anywhere I can find a quiet canyon. I'm an outdoor-type person. That's why I like off-road racing, which I did for many years. I enjoy being outside and in the sun. I would like to work at something outside.

I was at Riverside when my dad was killed. I was eighteen and with a friend. We were driving a rental car around practicing parking and doing things to irritate Les Richter. I remember looking down towards Turn Nine and I saw a ball of flame going through the air. I knew right then what had happened. We drove over, but we weren't the first ones there. Carroll Smith was there with some of the other guys. I remember seeing the car burning, but I didn't see my dad. I thought he was in the car, but everyone was just kind of standing around. I said why don't we put the fire out and get him out of the car. Carroll said that he was not in the car. I asked, "Where is he?" I expected to see him standing around somewhere. Carroll pointed over somewhere to the right and there he was on his back, all mangled. I couldn't bring myself to go over and look real closely, but I could see his helmet was off and his head was messed up. One of his legs was bent up backwards. It was a pretty gnarly time.

I didn't want to, but Carroll and I drove around the track to try to see if we could figure out what had happened. Towards the end of the straight, we could see marks from only one set of tires. They had locked up and the marks went off towards the end of the embankment. It looked as if the transmission had locked or just the rear brakes locked. The tire marks swerved off towards the inside of Turn Nine.

To get home that day, we had to fight rush-hour traffic. When I got home, I had never seen so many people in my life. Everyone had dropped whatever they were doing and came to our house to see if they could be some sort of support. I came in and both my mom and I burst into tears. It was a sad time.

When my dad was killed, we were right at the point when we were just starting to transition from a father - son relationship to becoming friends. So I really miss that feeling of knowing him as a friend. I wish I could have had that experience. Before that time, he was pretty one-sided about how he wanted things. He was kind of domineering, I guess. At that point, I started to ask him technical questions, things that he could relate to. I wish I could have known him as a friend.

The photographs on this and the previous page are from the Peter Miles collection. The one of Peter and his father was taken by Dean Batchelor and is from the Ron Kellogg collection.

EPILOGUE

When I started thinking about doing this book, the first thing I wanted to do was get in touch with Peter Miles. Peter is the only offspring of Ken and Mollie. For one reason or another, he wasn't in contact with sources available to me.

While doing research at *Road & Track*, their librarian, Jane Barrett, mentioned that there was a Dutch fellow who was a friend of Peter's. She gave me his e-mail address and I wrote him explaining my project and my desire to talk with Peter. My e-mail was forwarded to Peter and, in due time, he called me. It turned out that Peter was living in Santa Ana and working at a classic-car restoration shop in the San Fernando Valley (a hefty commute).

On October 18, 2003, I visited Peter at his apartment. We talked about our families and their relationship and Peter recorded his remembrances. He had a storage box brim full of photographs and other memorabilia. We went through the collection and some of the photographs are incorporated here.

One of the treasures Peter found in his box of memories was what has to be the earliest photograph of his father. Taken in 1918, it shows Ken's father, Eric, in his WWI British Army uniform and his mother, Clarice.

As we talked, we discovered something rather serendipitous. Some years after Ken's death, Mollie remarried. My stepmother, who was Mollie's confidant, had told me about it, but she never mentioned the husband's name and I never met him.

Peter told me his stepfather's name was Paul Hinkley. I said, "That's strange, a fellow worked for me at one time with the same name." Peter mentioned that he and Hinkley didn't get along and described him. "Whoa I, remarked, he sounds like my former employee!" Hinkley was a West Point graduate who was at the Academy a few years before me. Paul had gone into the Air Force and became a fighter pilot. He retired and bought a house near the Miles home. As Peter told me more details, it became obvious that the Paul Hinkley Mollie married and the one I knew were one and the same.

Mollie Miles (left), my stepmother, Betsy (center) and my sister, Lisa at a party at Betsy's mother's home in Pasadena. *Snapshot by Ken Miles*

I met Paul at a West Point Association gathering and, to make a long story short, gave him a job. During the late sixties, in addition to my motion picture production company, I had a sound studio and a small machine shop making modifications to film equipment. I was fully occupied directing and producing, so I needed someone to take care of the machine shop business. Paul fit the bill. After a year or so, for technological reasons (the products we were making become obsolete due to videotape), we disbanded the machine-shop enterprise. (As an aside, Sonny Bono was one of our customers.) I never saw Paul again. Mollie and Paul were married in 1971 and Mollie died two years later. Paul followed her in death shortly thereafter.

When I got home from my visit with Peter, I rummaged through an old scrapbook and came up with this snapshot taken by my wife, Alicia, on the occasion of my birthday on January 8, 1970. It shows some of my crew with Paul Hinkley on the left. Next to Paul is Ron (sound technician), Irv Nafshun (sound mixer), Paul Dexler (writer), yours truly, Greg (cameraman), Raphael (machinist), and Carlos Chiri (assistant cameraman and my brother-in-law).

I took this photograph of Peter at a Fabulous Fifties Association get-together on October 25, 2003. At the time, Peter was 55 years old. When Peter was younger, there seemed to me to be little resemblance between him and his father. But in later, years, Peter has, I think,

grown to look more and more like Ken. Among Peter's collection, we found a proof sheet of headshots Peter said were taken for a passport. So I scanned the contact print and have printed them here side-by-side. The photograph of Ken was taken while he was in his late forties.

Happily, I have been able to get Peter involved with our Fabulous Fifties Association and he seems to enjoy it. I know that the many friends and competitors of his father enjoy having him. Peter is happily married to his second wife, Linda. He has one offspring, a daughter, Jaine, by his first marriage. She was 19 in the fall of 2003 and a student at American Rivers College.

To end on an amusing note, please turn the previous page and notice the photograph of Mollie, Ken and Peter. There is a Siamese cat sitting on Peter's lap. The cat was the family pet. On one occasion when I was visiting at the Miles home on Sunday Trail, I needed to go to the bathroom. When I arrived at the facility, I found the cat sitting on the toilet doing it's duty. It turned out that Ken had taught this to the cat. Unfortunately, he couldn't get the cat to flush.

While I was visiting Linda and Peter, I noticed that their family pet is also a cat. I asked Peter if he had taught the cat to sit on the toilet. He replied that sadly, he had not been able to acquire this skill from his father. Apparently it is one acquired rather than inherited.

APPENDIX: KEN MILES' RACE RECORD

Date	Venue	Car	Entrant/Owner	Finish	Remarks
1949					
4/23	Silverstone	Frazer-Nash	Ken Miles	2nd in the over-3000cc class	
5/22	Prescott Hill Climb	Frazer-Nash	Ken Miles	1st in the over-3000cc class; time: 51.59 seconds	
6/12	Prescott Hill Climb	Frazer-Nash	Ken Miles	2nd in the over-3000cc class	
6/19	Silverstone	Frazer-Nash	Ken Miles	DNF (Lost chain whilst in 3rd.)	
7/2	Silverstone	Frazer-Nash	Ken Miles	3rd in class and set fastest lap of the event at 71.44 mph.	
7/17	Prescott Hill Climb	Frazer-Nash	Ken Miles	No reported results for Miles in the press. A rainy day.	
1950					
5/20	Prescott Hill Climb	Frazer-Nash	Ken Miles	No reported results for Miles in the press.	
6/6	Shelsley Walsh	Frazer-Nash	Ken Miles	No reported results for Miles in the press.	
7/7	Prescott Hill Climb	Frazer-Nash	Ken Miles	No reported results for Miles in the press.	
7/23	Great Auclum H.C.	Triangle Special	Ken Miles	2nd in class.	
9/10	Prescott Hill Climb	Frazer-Nash	Ken Miles	Press reported a Mr. Disney in the Miles Frazer-Nash; he crashed	
1951					
5/19	Silverstone	Frazer-Nash	Ken Miles	Vintage Club Event. Miles not listed in *Autosport*.	
7/28	Great Auclum H.C.	Alfa Romeo	Ken Miles	5th in class #2 in the "Sprint"	
1952					
4/20	Pebble Beach	MGTD	Gough Ind.	17th in the under-1500cc main event	
5/31	Golden Gate	MGTD	Gough Ind.	9th in the under-1500cc main event	
6/21	Carrell Speedway	MGTD	Gough Ind.	7th in first heat	
7/19-20	Torrey Pines	MGTD	Gough Ind.	5th in under 1500cc main event in absolutely stock TD!	
8/24	Stockton	MGTD	Gough Ind.	9th overall, 2nd in class (*Road & Track*: "Remarkable")	
11/9	Madera	MGTD	Gough Ind.	7th in the under-1500cc main event	
12/13-14	Torrey Pines	MGTD	Gough Ind.	4th in under-1500cc main event (Roger Barlow: "Tremendous")	
1953					
1/18	Carrell Speedway	MGTD 1500	Gough Ind.	1st trophy dash, 3rd main event	
4/18-19	Pebble Beach	MG Special R-1	Miles/Gough Ind.	1st under 1500cc semi-main (wins first race R-1 is entered!)	
5/3	Phoenix	MG Special R-1	Miles/Gough Ind.	1st under 1500cc semi-main,	
5/30	Golden Gate	MG Special R-1	Miles/Gough Ind.	1st under 1500cc semi-main, 3rd overall main event	
6/28	Stockton	MG Special R-1	Miles/Gough Ind.	1st under 1500cc semi-main, 2rd overall main event	
7/12	Chino	MG Special R-1	Miles/Gough Ind.	1st under 1500cc semi-main, 2rd overall main event	
8/16	Moffett Field	MG Special R-1	Miles/Gough Ind.	1st under 1500cc semi-main, 3rd overall main event	
9/6	Santa Barbara	MG Special R-1	Miles/Gough Ind.	1st under 1500cc semi-main, 5th overall main event	
9/20	Madera	MG Special R-1	Miles/Gough Ind.	1st under 1500cc semi-main, 4th overall main event	
10/3-4	Terminal Island	MG Special R-1	Miles/Gough Ind.	1st under 1500cc semi-main, 2nd overall main event	
11/6	March Field	MG Special R-1	Miles/Gough Ind.	1st under 1500cc semi-main	

1954

Date	Location	Car	Entrant	Result
1/23-24	Palm Springs	MG Special R-1	Miles/Gough Ind.	1st under 1500cc-semi-main, 3rd overall main event
3/21	Bakersfield	MG Special R-1	Miles/Gough Ind.	1st under 1500cc-semi-main, 1st overall main event
4/10-11	Pebble Beach	MG Special R-1	Miles/Gough Ind.	DNF: engine blew up while in the lead
5/8-9	Willow Springs	MGTF	Gough Industries	1st Heat No. 1, 2nd Heat No. 2
6/5	Golden Gate	Troutman-Barnes Spl	Troutman & Barnes	DNF (While running 3rd overall.)
6/5	Golden Gate	MGTF 1500	Gough Ind.	5th in the under-1500cc main event I
7/3-4	Torrey Pines	Troutman-Barnes Spl	Troutman & Barnes	1st Saturday main event, DNF Sunday (Yedor 1st u/1500 in R-1)
7/3-3	Torrey Pines	MGTF	Gough Ind.	?
9/4	Santa Barbara	MGTF	Gough Ind.	7th overall Saturday u/1500 main event
9-5	Santa Barbara	Troutman-Barnes Spl	Troutman & Barnes	2nd overall main event
10/16-17	Palm Springs	Formula 3 Cooper	Ken Miles	3rd overall, formula race
10/16-17	Palm Springs	Troutman-Barnes Sp	Troutman & Barnes	DNF
10/16-17	Palm Springs	Siata Spyder	Al Coppel	3rd overall, u/1500 semi-main

1955

Date	Location	Car	Entrant	Result
2/13	Willow Springs	MG Special R-2	Miles/Gough Ind.	DNS: (First outing. "Running like a sewer.)
3/26-27	Palm Springs	MG Special R-2	Miles/Gough Ind.	1st under 1500 semi-main, 1st consolation race, 7th main
4/16-17	Pebble Beach	MG Special R-2	Miles/Gough Ind.	1st under 1500 semi-main, 3rd overall main event
5/28-29	Santa Barbara	MG Special R-2	Miles/Gough Ind.	1st Saturday under 1500 semi-main, 1st Sunday semi-main
5/28-29	Santa Barbara	Austin-Healey 100S	Clem Atwater	9th oa, 1st cl Saturday, 10th oa, 3rd cl Sunday in production race
6/11	Le Mans	MG EX 182	MG Cars Ltd.	12th overall, 5th in class (co-driver: John Lockkett)
7/31	Seattle Seafair	Ferrari 375	Allen Guiberson	3rd overall (Behind Shelby and Hill.)
9/3-4	Santa Barbara	MG Special R-2	Miles/Gough Ind.	2nd Saturday under 1500 semi-main, 1st Sunday semi-main
9/3-4	Santa Barbara	4.9 Ferrari	Tony Parravano	3rd Saturday main event, DNF Sunday main event
10/1-2	Salinas	Lotus 1100cc	Scuderia Excelsior	2nd semi-main
10/22	Torrey Pines 6-Hour	MGA	Gough Industries	18th overall, 4th in cl Fp (co-driver: Cy Yedor)
10/23	Torrey Pines	MG Special R-2	Miles/Gough Ind.	1st under 1500 semi-main
10/30	Sacramento	MG Special R-2	Miles/Gough Ind.	2nd under 1500 main (Pete Lovely 1st in Pooper), 3rd main event
12/3-4	Palm Springs	Maserati 150S	Tony Parravano	1st Saturday u/1500 semi-main, 1st Sunday semi, 7th main event

1956

Date	Location	Car	Entrant	Result
1/14	Torrey Pines 6-Hour	Porsche 550	John von Neumann	Crashes car during practice. DNS for the 6-Hour race.
1/14	Torrey Pines 6-Hour	MGA	Gough Industries	3rd in class. Co-driver: Cy Yedor
1/15	Torrey Pines	Porsche 550	John Von Neumann	1st under 1500cc semi-main, 3rd overall main event
2/25-26	Palm Springs	Porsche 550	John Von Neumann	2nd under 1500cc semi-main, 3rd overall main event
3/17-18	Santa Barbara	Porsche 550	John Von Neumann	2nd under 1500cc semi-main, DNF main event
5/19-20	Bakersfield	Porsche 550	John Von Neumann	1st Saturday under 1500cc semi-main, 1st Sunday semi-main
6/23-24	Pomona	Porsche 550	John Von Neumann	1st Saturday semi-main, 2nd Sunday semi-main, 4th Sunday main
7/21-22	Montgomery Field	Porsche 550	John Von Neumann	1st Saturday semi-main, 1st Sunday semi-main, 3rd Sunday main
9/1-2	Santa Barbara	Porsche 550	John Von Neumann	1st Saturday semi-main, 1st Sunday semi-main
9/30	Sacramento	Porsche 550	John Von Neumann	3rd semi-main, 6th main event (pushed car over the line)
10/20-21	Pomona	Porsche-Cooper	Dick Troutman	1st Saturday semi-main, 2nd Sunday semi-main

11/17-18	Paramount Ranch	Porsche-Cooper	Dick Troutman	1st Saturday semi-main, 1st Sunday semi-main, 1st main event
12/8	Nassau	Porsche-Cooper	John Von Neumann	1st in class, 4th overall (Porsche 4-cam engine)

1957

1/19-20	Pomona	Porsche-Cooper	John Von Neumann	1st Saturday semi-main, 1st Sunday semi-main, DNF main event
3/9-10	Paramount Ranch	Porsche 550	John Von Neumann	2nd Saturday semi-main, 2nd Sunday semi-main (Drake 1st)
3/23	Sebring	Porsche 550	Jean Pierre Kunstle	2nd in class, 9th overall (co-driver: Jean Pierre Kunstle)
4/6-7	Palm Springs	Porsche RS	John Von Neumann	2nd Saturday semi-main, 1st Sunday semi-main
4/21	Hawaii	Porsche 550	John Von Neumann	1st in class, 5th overall
4	Puebla, Mexico	Porsche 550	John Von Neumann	2nd overall (1st Ricardo Rodriguez)
5/4-5	Hourglass Field	Porsche	John Von Neumann	1st Saturday semi-main, 1st Sunday semi-main
5/18-19	Santa Barbara	Porsche	John Von Neumann	2nd Saturday semi-main, 1st Sunday semi-main
6/15-16	Paramount Ranch	Porsche	John Von Neumann	1st main event but DISQ for stopping for a drink, lapped all
7/27-28	Pomona	Porsche RS	John Von Neumann	1st semi-main
8/31-9/1	Santa Barbara	Porsche RS	John Von Neumann	1st semi-main
10/26-27	Pomona	Porsche RS	John Von Neumann	2nd Saturday semi-main, 1st Sunday semi-main
12/77-8	Paramount Ranch	Porsche RS	John Von Neumann	2nd Saturday semi-main, 1st Sunday semi-main

1958

2/8-9	Pomona	Porsche 550	Otto Zipper	3rd Saturday semi-main, 2nd Sunday semi-main
3/22	Sebring	Porsche RS	Jean Pierre Kunstle	DNF (co-driver: Jean Pierre Kunstle)
4/6	Avandaro, Mexico	Porsche	Otto Zipper	2nd overall
5/31-6/1	Santa Barbara	Porsche RS	Otto Zipper	2nd Saturday semi-main, 2nd Sunday semi-main (Jack McAfee 1st)
6/15	Arrowhead Hill Climb	Talbot-Lago GP	Otto Zipper	3rd fastest time of the day
6/28-29	Riverside	Porsche RS	Otto Zipper	3rd Saturday semi-main, 2nd Sunday semi-main
6/29	Riverside	Talbot-Lago GP	Zipper-de Goldsmith	4th main event
8/30-31	Santa Barbara	Porsche RS	Otto Zipper	DISQ Saturday semi-main, 1st Sunday semi-main under 2000cc
8/30-31	Santa Barbara	4.4 Ferrari 121LM	Jack Brumby	4th overall main event (Ex-Parravano Ferrari)
10/11	Riverside USGP	Porsche RS	Otto Zipper	2nd in u/1500 class (Jean Behra first)
11/9	Laguna Seca	Porsche RS	Otto Zipper	2nd in under-1500cc main event
11/22	Pomona 6-Hour	D-Type Jaguar	Carlysle Blackwell	1st overall (co-driver: Carlysle Blackwell)
11/23	Pomona	Porsche RS	Otto Zipper	1st overall main event

1959

2/1	Pomona	Porsche RS	Otto Zipper	3rd overall main event
3/8	Pomona EX GP	Porsche RS	Otto Zipper	1st overall in USAC professional race
3/21	Sebring	Porsche RSK	Otto Zipper	8th overall (co-driver: Jack McAfee)
4/26	Avandaro Mexico	Porsche RS	Otto Zipper	1st
5/31-6/1	Santa Barbara	Porsche RSK	Otto Zipper	1st Saturday semi-main, 1st Sunday semi-main, DISQ main event
7/18-19	Riverside USAC	Porsche RSK	Otto Zipper	2nd overall main event professional race
9/6	Santa Barbara	Porsche RSK	Otto Zipper	1st overall main event
10/11	Riverside Times GP	Porsche RSK	Otto Zipper	3rd overall main event professional race

1960

2/14	Willow Springs	Porsche RSK	Otto Zipper	2nd overall main event

Date	Location	Car	Entrant	Result
4/3	Riverside EX GP	Porsche RS60	Otto Zipper	2nd overall, 1st in class
5/1	Vacaville	Porsche RS60	Otto Zipper	1st in class, 4th overall
5/29	Santa Barbara	MBZ-Chevy Spl	Chuck Porter	DNF (Running 2nd when engine trouble forced withdrawl.)
5/29	Santa Barbara	Stangulini FJR	Jean Pierre Kunstle	3rd in the formula race
6/5	Laguna Seca	Porsche RS60	Otto Zipper	1st overall
10/16	Riverside Times GP	Porsche RS60	Otto Zipper	13th overall, 2nd in class
10/23	Laguna Seca 1st HT	Porsche RS60	Otto Zipper	6th overall, 2nd in class
10/23	Laguna Seca 2nd HT	Porsche RS60	Otto Zipper	8th overall, 3rd in class
10/11-12	Riverside	Porsche RS60	Otto Zipper	2nd in class (LA Times GP)
11/6	Pomona	Dolphin FJR	Dolphin Engr. Co.	1st formula race
12/23	Las Vegas	Porsche RS60	Otto Zipper	DNF
12/23	Las Vegas	Dolphin FJ	Dolphin Engr. Co.	2nd in formula race

r

1961

Date	Location	Car	Entrant	Result
1/8	Pomona	Porsche RS60	Otto Zipper	2nd overall main event
1/15	Mexico City	Dolphin FJ	Dolphin Engr. Co.	DNF
3/12	Pomona	Dolphin FJ	Dolphin Engr. Co.	2nd formula race
4/23	Las Vegas	Porsche RS60	Otto Zipper	DNF
4/16	Stockton	Dolphin FJ	Dolphin Engr. Co.	DNF
6/11	Laguna Seca	Porsche RS60	Dan Hermann	4th overall, 1st in class
6/25	Indianapolis	Porsche	Frank Zillner	3rd overall (Indianapolis Raceway Park
7/2	Colorado Pro	Porache RS61	Frank Zillner	1st in Heat No. 1, 2nd in Heat No. 2, Miles overall winner
7/9	Pomona	Dolphin FJ	Dolphin Engr. Co.	5th formula race
7/9	Pomona	Sunbeam Alpiine	Rootes Motors	4th production race
8/12	Riverside Oval	Sunbeam Alpine	Rootes Motors	5th in F Production
9/24	Reno	Porsche RS61	Frank Zillner	1st class, 3rd overall (At Stead AFB)
9/3	Santa Barbara	Porsche RS	Vasek Polak	1st overall main event
9/3	Santa Barbara	Sunbeam Alpine	Rootes Motors	2nd production race
10/15	Riverside	Porsche RS61	Frank Zillner	2nd class, 7th overall (Times GP)
10/22	Laguna Seca	Porsche RS61	Frank Zillner	2st class, 9th overall, first heat
10/22	Laguna Seca	Porsche RS61	Frank Zillner	3nd class, 11th overall, second heat

1962

Date	Location	Car	Entrant	Result
3/24	Sebring	Sunbeam Alpine	Roots Motors	DNF
5/27	Santa Barbara	Ferrari 500TRC	Otto Zipper	1st overall main event
5/27	Santa Barbara	Sunbeam Alpine	Rootes Motors	1st in F Production
6/10	Laguna Seca	Sunbeam Alpine	Rootes Motors	1st production race
6/23	Riverside 6-Hour	Ferrari SWB	Otto Zipper	1st overall (co-driver: Bob Drake)
6/24	Riverside Sprint	Ferrari SWB	Otto Zipper	1st overall production car race
7/22	Pomona	Ferrari SWB	Otto Zipper	1st overall production car race
8/19	Pomona	Porache RS61	Otto Zipper	2nd overall main event
8/19	Pomona	Sunbeam Alpine	Rootes Motors	1st production race
9/22	Reno	Ferrari SWB	Bill Harrah	1st overall production car race (Ex Estes-Zipper car)

Date	Location	Car	Entrant	Result
9/23	Reno	Ferrari 500TRC	Otto Zipper	DNF
10/14	Riverside	Maserati T-61	Maserati Reps	6th overall (Times GP)
10/21	Laguna Seca	Maserati T-61	Maserati Reps	DNF
10/21	Laguna Seca	Ferrari SWB	Bill Harrah	1st overall production car race
1963				
2/2-3	Riverside	Cobra	Shelby American	2nd (Dave McDonald first in another Cobra.)
2/2-3	Riverside	Porsche RS61	Otto Zipper	2nd overall
3/3	Dodger Stadium	Cobra	Shelby American	2nd
3/3	Dodger Stadium	Porsche RS61	Otto Zipper	1st overall
3/23	Sebring	Cobra	Shelby American	DNF (co driver: Lou Spencer)
5/26	Pensacola, FL	Porsche ?	Riesentoter	1st (co-driver: Bob Holbert)
5/26	Pensacola, FL	Cobra	Shelby American	DNF
6/9	Laguna Seca	Cobra	Shelby American	1st GT class, 9th overall
6/23	Riverside	Dolphin-Porsche	Otto Zipper	2nd overall
6/30	Watkins Glen	Cobra	Shelby American	2nd overall, Manufacturer's Championship
6/30	Watkins Glen DC	Cobra	Shelby American	3rd overall. Driver's Championship
7/7	Lake Garnett	Cobra	Shelby American	1st overall
7/14	Pomona	Dolphin-Porsche	Otto Zipper	DNF
7/21	Kent, WA	Cobra	Shelby American	5th overall, 2nd in class, Manufacturer's Championship
7/21	Kent, WA DC	Cobra	Shelby American	5th overall, Driver's Championship
9/5	Road America 500	Cobra	Shelby American	2nd overall (co-driver: Bob Holbert)
9/14	Bridgehampton	Cobra	Shelby American	2nd overall (Dan Gurney won in another Cobra.)
9/22	Mid-Ohio	Cobra	Shelby American	2nd overall, Manufacturer's Championship
9/22/63	Mid-Ohio	Cobra	Shelby American	1st overall, Driver's Championship
9/28	Mosport	Cobra	Comstock Team	2nd GT class, 7th overall
11/3	Riverside	Ford Galaxie	Fred Lorenzen	11th (Miles in 6th when Lorenzen took over.)
12/8	Nassau	Cobra	Shelby American	DNF
12/14-15	Dodger Stadium	Porsche RS60	Otto Zipper	1st overall
1964				
3/1	Augusta	Cobra	Shelby American	1st overall, Manufacturer's Championship
3/1	Augusta	Cobra	Shelby American	6th overall, 1st production class, Driver's Championship
3/21	Sebring	427 Cobra Prototype	Shelby American	DNF (scored as 47th overall) (Co-driver: John Morton)
4/5	Pensacola	Cobra	Shelby American	1st overall, Manufacturer's Championship
4/5	Pensacola	King Cobra	Shelby American	DNF, Driver's Championship
4/19	Phoenix	Cobra	Shelby American	1st GT class, 7th overall
4/26	Riverside	Cobra	Shelby American	2nd overall, Manufacturer's Championship
5/19	Kent	Cobra	Shelby American	1st overall, Manufacturer's Championship
5/19	Kent	Cobra	Shelby American	4th overall, Driver's Championship
5/3	Laguna Seca	Lotus 23	?	18th overall, 2nd in class
5/3	Laguna Seca	Cobra	Shelby American	2nd overall, production race

Date	Track	Car	Team	Result
6/8	Mosport	Cobra	Shelby American	DNF
6/28	Watkins Glen	Cobra	Shelby American	1st overall, Manufacturer's Championship
6/28	Watkins Glen	Cobra	Shelby American	5th overall, Driver's Championship
7/19	Greenwood	Cobra	Shelby American	1st GT class, 4th overall, USRRC
8/30	Mid Ohio	Cobra	Shelby American	4th overall
9/9	Meadowdale	Cobra	Shelby American	1st overall, Manufacturer's Championship
9/9	Meadowdale	Cobra	Shelby American	5th overall, Driver's Championship
9/12	Road America	Sunbeam Tiger	Sherby American	2nd 200 mi. "Badger 200" race
9/13	Road America	Cobra	Shelby American	1st GT class, 2nd overall (Co-driver: Al Holbert)
9/20	Bridgehampton	Cobra	Shelby American	1st GT class, 4th overall
10/11	Riverside	Cobra	Shelby American	DNF
11/29	Nassau	390 Cobra Prototype	Shelby American	DNF, Tourist Trophy

1965

Date	Track	Car	Team	Result
2/28	Daytona	GT-40	Shelby American	1st overall, 24-Hours (Co-driver: Lloyd Ruby)
3/27	Sebring	GT-40	Shelby American	2nd overall, 12-Hours (Co-driver: Bruce McLaren)
4/25	Monza	GT-40	Shelby American	3rd overall, 1000km (Co-driver: Bruce McLaren)
5/2	Riverside	Cobra	Shelby American	2nd overall, Manufacturer's Championship
5/2	Riverside	427 Cobra Prototype	Shelby American	DNF, Driver's Championship
5/9	Laguna Seca	Cobra	Shelby American	1st overall, Manufacturer's Championship
6/19-20	Le Mans 24	GT-40 MkII	Shelby American	DNF (Co-driver: Bruce McLaren)
11/?	Australia	427 Cobra	Shelby American	DNF

1966

Date	Track	Car	Team	Result
2/5-6	Daytona	GT-40 MkII	Shelby American	1st overall, 24-Hours (Co-driver: Lloyd Ruby)
3/26	Sebring	GT-40 MkII XI	Shelby American	1st overall, 12-Hours (Co-driver: Lloyd Ruby)
4/24	Las Vegas	Porsche 906	Otto Zipper	6th overall, 1st in class
5/8	Laguna Seca	Porsche 906	Otto Zipper	5th overall, 1st in class
5/22	Bridgehampton	Porsche 906	Otto Zipper	DNS
6/18-19	Le Mans	GT-40	Shelby American	2nd overall, 24-Hours (Co-driver: Dennis Hulme)
6/26	Watkins Glen	Porsche 906	Otto Zipper	DNS*
8/17	Riverside testing	Ford J Car	Ford Motor Co.	Ken Miles killed when car disintegrated.

1968

Date	Track	Car	Team	Result
10/12/68	Laguna Seca	Memorial		Ken Miles Memorial Race (winner: Lou Sell in his Eagle Formula 5000)

*According to Bob Kovacik in the September 1966 issue of *Sports Car Graphic*, "The Porsche Carrera Sixes of Otto Zipper, which had won all the USRRC under-two-liter races that season, were withdrawn and put up for sale the day before the race. The action was taken after Ken Miles 'blew' an engine during the Friday practice session and a replacement was not available. Zipper claimed his reason for withdrawing was because of lack of support from the Southern California distributor (Von Neumann). 'I have no complaints about the Porsche factory,' he said."

Autographed Portraits of Race Legends of the Fabulous Fifties
by Art Evans

Each picture is printed on 8x10 double-weight Agfa photographic paper. On the back of each print is a signed and dated certificate attesting to the validity of the autograph. Additionally, prints are mounted in an acid-free double matte and signed by the photographer.

Bob Bondurant
Tony Adamowicz
Sir Jack Brabham
Chuck Daigh
Vic Edelbrock, Jr.
John Fitch
George Follmer
Jerry Grant
Dick Guldstrand
David Hobbs
Phil Hill
Ed Hugus
Parnelli Jones
Bruce Kessler
Oscar Koveleski
Bill Krause
Pete Lovely
Jack McAfee
John Morton
Al Moss
Sir Stirling Moss
Bill Murphy
Augie Pabst
Jim Parkinson
Scooter Patrick

Bill Pollack
Andy Porterfield
Joe Playan
Brian Redman
Carroll Shelby
Bobby Unser
Rodger Ward
Cy Yedor

Specials: Hill and Shelby racing nose to nose in Ferraris at the '56 Palm Springs.(two autographs)

Brabham racing a F1 Cooper at the GP of Riverside in 1961

Unautographed:
Briggs Cunningham
Bill Devin
Dennis Hulme
Juan Manuel Fangio
Paul O'Shea
Bill Stroppe

Art Evans, the author of this book, is also the author of nine books about photography and cameras. A celebrated photographer, his prints have been exhibited numerous times including a one-person show at Lincoln Center. He started his photo career shooting sports car races during the fabulous fifties. He is a contributor to a number of magazines including *Road & Track*, *Vintage Motorsport* and *Shutterbug*.

Each autographed print is $49. Unautographed ones are $39. The Hill & Shelby is $69.

Add $9 each shipping & handling. Payment by check, money order or credit card. VISA or MasterCard: list acct. #, exp. date, name on card, card billing address and shipping address.

Photo Data Research
Fabulous-fifties.com
310-540-8068

RACE LEGENDS OF THE FABULOUS FIFTIES
a book by Art Evans

The decade of the fifties is remembered by automobile racing enthusiasts as an era of creativity and non-stop action. Some of its flavor has been memorialized in a new book by Art Evans, *Race Legends of the Fabulous Fifties.* The book is hardbound with 136 pages in an 8½x11-inch format, is printed on 100-pound glossy paper and has an MSRP of $49.

There are many books about historic and vintage cars, but this one is centered around people. The project started with a collection of portraits by the author, not only a celebrated photographer, but also a friend of each subject. Almost all of the fifty-one portraits are contemporary, taken since the middle 1980s. Each black and white portrait is printed full page on high-quality coated paper. On each opposing page is a mini-biography and photographs from the fifties. In many cases, there are pictures showing what the people looked like during that era.

Included among the featured drivers involved in the sport are, Max Balchowsky, Bob Bondurant, Sir Jack Brabham, Briggs Cunningham, James Dean, Bill Devin, Steve Earle, Juan Manuel Fangio, John Fitch, Dan Gurney,

Jim Hall, Sam Hanks, Phil Hill, Dennis Hulme, Parnelli Jones, Jack McAfee, Ken Miles, Sir Stirling Moss, Paul O'Shea, Vasek Polak, Brian Redman, Lance Reventlow, Carroll Shelby, Bobby Unser and Rodger Ward.

More than a biography of each subject, the author recounts some very personal remembrances as well as amusing anecdotes. Carroll Shelby, in his introduction to the book says, "The fifties was the greatest time to be a race driver. Art, I'm really proud that you have put this book together." Chris Economaki in *National Speed Sport News* says, "It's a superb volume. Great copy and great photos of its subjects plus data on the circuits of the era."

Another feature is a section on legendary race venues of the past. Discussions of competitions on public highways and city streets are illustrated with examples like Watkins Glen, Bridgehampton, the Sandberg Hill-Climb, Palm Springs, the Mexican Road Race, Elkhart Lake, Pebble Beach and Torrey Pines. All are liberally illustrated with period photographs.

A final section consists of advertisements reproduced from event programs and periodicals of the fifties. Some feature businesses in which various race legends were involved. They provide a fascinating glimpse into the past. Some are quite rare and seldom, if ever, seen since the fifties.

Two previous books by the author about the fifties met with critical success and are sold out. Evans' books are not only enthralling histories, but also collectable in themselves. Evans knows whereof he speaks. Art is not only a writer and photographer, but also was a sports car racer himself.

Evans' first book about the fifties was a collection of portraits of Southern California legends. A margin below each full-page portrait provides space for an autograph. Many of those lucky enough to obtain a copy have acquired collections of signatures from the featured racing greats. Undoubtedly, this new book will serve much the same function.

LIMITED EDITION, ORDER TODAY

Order from your favorite automobilia book store (Autobooks, Automobilia Collectibles, Green Mountain, Menoshire (UK), RaceLegends.com, TAD Corp. (Japan), Transportation Book Service.

Or buy directly: $49 +$9 s&h. Photo Data Research, 800 S. Pacific Coast Hwy., Redondo Beach, CA 90277, Email: photodataresearch@yahoo.com, Fax 310-373-5988. Check, MasterCard or VISA. Give account number, expiration date, name on card, card billing address and shipping address if different. Request author autograph and inscription. Delivery via U.S. Priority Mail.

Key to portraits: Top left to right: Juan Manuel Fangio, Sir Jack Brabham, Briggs Cunningham, Phil Hill. Bottom: left to right: John Fitch, Denny Hulme, Bobby Unser, Dan Gurney. All portraits were taken by the author within the past ten years.

THE FABULOUS FIFTIES ASSOCIATION

During the later part of the fifties, I was closely associated with OCee Ritch, both socially and in business. Separately, both of us had small public relations and advertising enterprises, so we merged, thinking the whole might be greater than the parts. During the seventies we worked together in the film business. One day while we were lunching at the Blarney Castle restaurant, its proprietor, Rudy Cleye, joined us at our table. We thought it might be fun to get together with others of those involved in the fifties sports car racing scene.

Rudy had a separate party room at his restaurant, so we set a date for a cocktail party and reserved the room. At this point, of course, there was only the three of us. So each of us got out our old address books and started to hunt folks down. I was happy that one of the first I was able to contact was Jack McAfee. One thing led to another and when the day came, there was quite a crowd. Reminiscences ran rampant!

A few years later, Bill Pollack had taken over the management of a substance recovery facility—Toum Est—in Venice. One day while I was visiting, Bill mentioned that he would like to have a fundraiser for the institution. I volunteered the invitation list from the Blarney Castle event and again, we had a large turnout. The following year, we had another fundraiser.

In 1985, I was instrumental in recreating the old Palm Springs Road Races as a vintage event. One of the races was the Fabulous Fifties exhibition. We gathered more than 50 of those who had competed at Palm Springs during the fifties, many in the same cars. And we had a party at my Palm Springs home. The *Los Angeles Times* was so impressed that the entire View Section was devoted to the event.

We had made a little money on the Palm Springs revival, so we blew the entire wad on a Christmas party at Mary Davis' Portofino Inn in Redondo Beach. Then Richie Ginther died and we had a wake at the Proud Bird near Los Angeles Airport. So the Fabulous Fifties "Association" was off and running.

At first, our get-togethers were usually lunches at the Proud Bird. When Pete Petersen decided to build his very own car museum, we started having a Christmas dinner there. Another regular event is our summer picnic at the Bothwell Ranch in Woodland Hills. A third tradition has evolved, a cocktail party at the Martine Inn on the Friday evening of the Monterey Historic weekend sponsored by Le Mans winner Ed Hugus, and the inn's proprietor, MG collector Don Martine.

Currently, we have settled into a routine of quarterly meetings plus the Monterey party. The "association" is not incorporated nor is it organized in any meaningful manner. New "members" are acquired by being nominated by old members. There are no dues. There is a newsletter, which is supported by voluntary donations.

The head honcho of this non-organization is one Bill Pollack, he of Allard fame. The treasurer is Alice Hanks (yes, Sam's Alice) and the secretary and newsletter editor is yours truly. Cy Yedor and Ann Bothwell round out the group that performs the hopefully very minimal amount of governance.

At this writing, the association roster included more than 700 names. Many are those who drove, officiated, worked or governed during the fifties. Some are those who were then on the other side of the snow fence. More and more are the descendants of those who were active during the decade.

The association started as an informal outgrowth of the Southern California's California Sports Car Club and the Los Angeles Region of the SCCA. As time has gone by, members from all over the country have been added such as Augie Pabst in the mid-west and John Fitch in the east. Sir Stirling Moss is one of a rather large group of European members while Sir Jack Brabham represents down under.

In addition to social events, the association maintains an archive of member-donated fifties-era photographs, race programs, official race results and other documents including books and magazines.

New members who turned a wheel, wielded a wrench, waved a flag, clicked a camera or scribbled for publication, hung around the paddock or gripped the snow fence are welcome, as well as their descendents. Others who are nominated by a member are also welcome. There are no dues or initiation fees. The association is supported by voluntary donations. The proceeds of periodic auctions of donated memorabilia are also an important asset. Qualified individuals are invited to contact us at 310-540-8068, e-mail: f50s@yahoo.com

About the Author
ART EVANS

Art Evans has a varied and extensive background. He and his partner, OCee Ritch, represented the MG Mitten Co., Devin Enterprises, Gough Industries and other car-related organizations during the fifties. Evans and another partner, Richard Sherwin, published the *West Coast Sports Car Journal*, later the *Sports Car Journal* which, for a time, was the official magazine of the California Sports Car Club. Evans served a term as a director of the Los Angeles Region of the Sports Car Club of America and published a number of fifties-era event programs.

Art drove a number of different cars during the fifties. His first race was in an MGTD at Palm Springs. He soon acquired an MG Special and then a succession of XK120 Jaguars. At the end of the decade, he campaigned the first Devin SS. Evans Industries was the exclusive distributor for Devin cars.

In the sixties, Evans turned to education and became an assistant professor and chair of the Photography Department at Orange Coast College in Costa Mesa, California. He became a leader in educational media, served as an officer in the Association for Educational Communications and Technology and was the principal investigator for a U.S. Department of Education research grant.

Turning to motion pictures during the seventies, including a seven-year stint at Paramount Communications as vice president for production, Art accumulated a large number of credits and awards including the George Washington Medal from the Freedoms Foundation. His still photographs have been featured in numerous shows including a solo exhibition at the Lincoln Center in New York.

Evans was educated at the U.S. Military Academy at West Point, California State University, the University of California at Los Angeles, the University of Southern California and California Western University. He has a bachelor, masters and doctoral degrees and three California teaching credentials.

The author of ten books about photography plus others on different subjects, Evans has written numerous articles for photography and automotive magazines as well as professional journals. His first book about motor sports, *The Fabulous Fifties, A Decade of Sports Car Racing in Southern California*, was published in 2001 to critical acclaim. This book is now out of print and copies are no longer available. In 2002, the second book in *The Fabulous Fifties* series, *Sports Car Races in Southern California*, was published. This book, also out of print and not available, describes more than 100 races at 22 venues. His third book, *Race Legends of the Fabulous Fifties* was published in 2003 and is in print.

During the eighties, Art began driving in vintage races. In 1985, he promoted a revival of the old Palm Springs Road Races followed by a succession of other vintage events including a vintage section at the Pikes Peak Hill Climb and open-road racing in Mexico.

Arthur Evans was born in 1934 in Santa Barbara, California. He served in the active Army, the California National Guard, the Army Reserve and as a Culver City reserve police officer. He lives in Redondo Beach with his wife, four children, a new grandchild, two dogs and three cats. In retirement, Evans pursues pastimes including writing about the fabulous fifties, creating memorabilia and serving as the secretary of The Fabulous Fifties Association. In addition he is associated with Race Legends, Inc., headed by Donn Gurney. The company represents some 40 legendary racing celebrities for appearances and endorsements.

A SPECIAL NOTE FROM ART EVANS

Like most of you, I believe in sharing some of my good fortune with others. But I'm very skeptical of most charities. I can't forget the newspaper story about the then president of United Way with his luxury condo in New York City, his limo and young girlfriends, all paid for with donations.

Through my friendship with Carroll Shelby, I have learned about a deserving charity that I can endorse without any qualms. It is the Carroll Shelby Children's Foundation. In fact, I have already put my money where my mouth is and I urge you to do likewise.

After years of heart-related difficulties that finally culminated in a successful heart transplant, Shel decided to provide assistance for young people who shared many of his afflictions. The charity he founded helps indigent children with acute coronary and kidney care.

At the conclusion of the 1960 season, Carroll had to retire from race driving due to his heart condition, but he had to wait years before receiving his heart transplant. He became keenly aware of the difficulties and expense involved in heart surgery and the often lengthy process to locate a suitable donor organ. He knew that many needy children would have their lives cut short without financial assistance.

Shel is personally involved in the selection of the children who receive his help. He has told me a number of stories about some of them. The first recipient, an infant named Leah Smith needed heart transplant medication in 1991. She was within days of dying because her parents didn't have the money. Leah is a healthy teenager today and on her way to the pre-Olympic Trials as a figure skater.

Carroll himself donates money plus the proceeds from his appearance and autograph fees. Donations are the only source of funding. The number of children who can be helped depends on you and others like you. More than 95% of all receipts go directly to beneficiaries. Only approximately 5% goes to administrative costs. Carroll himself accepts no reimbursement nor does he charge rent for office space and overhead.

Please get out your pen NOW and write a check to the Carroll Shelby Children's Foundation and mail it to Carroll at 19021 S. Figueroa St., Gardena, CA 90248. Or call (310) 327-5072 to use your credit

card. Your donation is tax deductible. The foundation is a Nonprofit Public Benefit Corporation. The Federal ID number is 95-4342625. You can visit on the internet: www.shelbychildrensfoundation.org.

Also, please urge others to join in this effort. Try to encourage any corporations you may be associated with to give some consideration to this worthy cause. And what could be more worthy than helping to keep children alive? One may grow up to be a Louis Pasteur, Mother Teresa or an Olympic medallist!